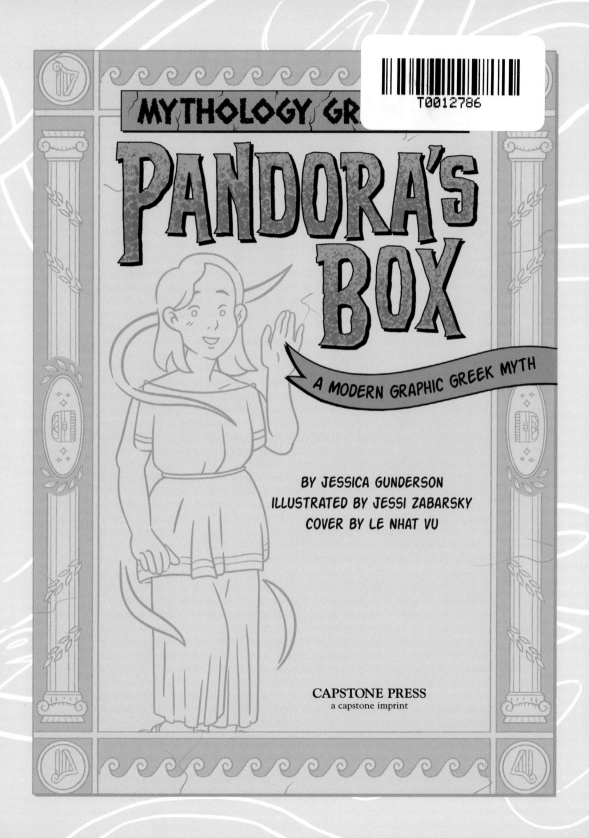

MYTHOLOGY GR

PANDORA'S BOX

A MODERN GRAPHIC GREEK MYTH

BY JESSICA GUNDERSON
ILLUSTRATED BY JESSI ZABARSKY
COVER BY LE NHAT VU

CAPSTONE PRESS
a capstone imprint

T0012786

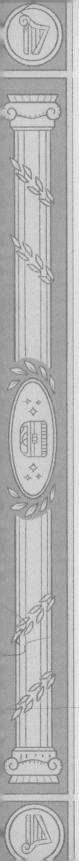

Published by Capstone Press, an imprint of Capstone
1710 Roe Crest Drive, North Mankato, Minnesota 56003
capstonepub.com

Copyright © 2024 by Capstone. All rights reserved. No part of this publication may
be reproduced in whole or in part, or stored in a retrieval system, or transmitted
in any form or by any means, electronic, mechanical, photocopying, recording,
or otherwise, without written permission of the publisher.

Library of Congress Cataloging-in-Publication Data is available
on the Library of Congress website.

ISBN: 9781669051091 (hardcover)
ISBN: 9781669051046 (paperback)
ISBN: 9781669051053 (ebook PDF)

Summary: No one holds a grudge like Zeus, king of the gods. So when Prometheus
steals fire to give to humans, Zeus is determined to get revenge. He sends
Pandora—the first mortal woman—to Earth with a box labeled DO NOT OPEN.
Can Pandora keep her curiosity under control? Learn the story behind this classic
Greek myth in a modern, graphic retelling.

Editorial Credits
Editor: Alison Deering; Designer: Jaime Willems; Media Researcher: Rebekah
Hubstenberger; Production Specialist: Whitney Schaefer

All internet sites appearing in back matter were available and accurate when
this book was sent to press.

Printed and bound in the USA. PO#5425

TABLE OF CONTENTS

CHAPTER 1

Such Demanding Gods!

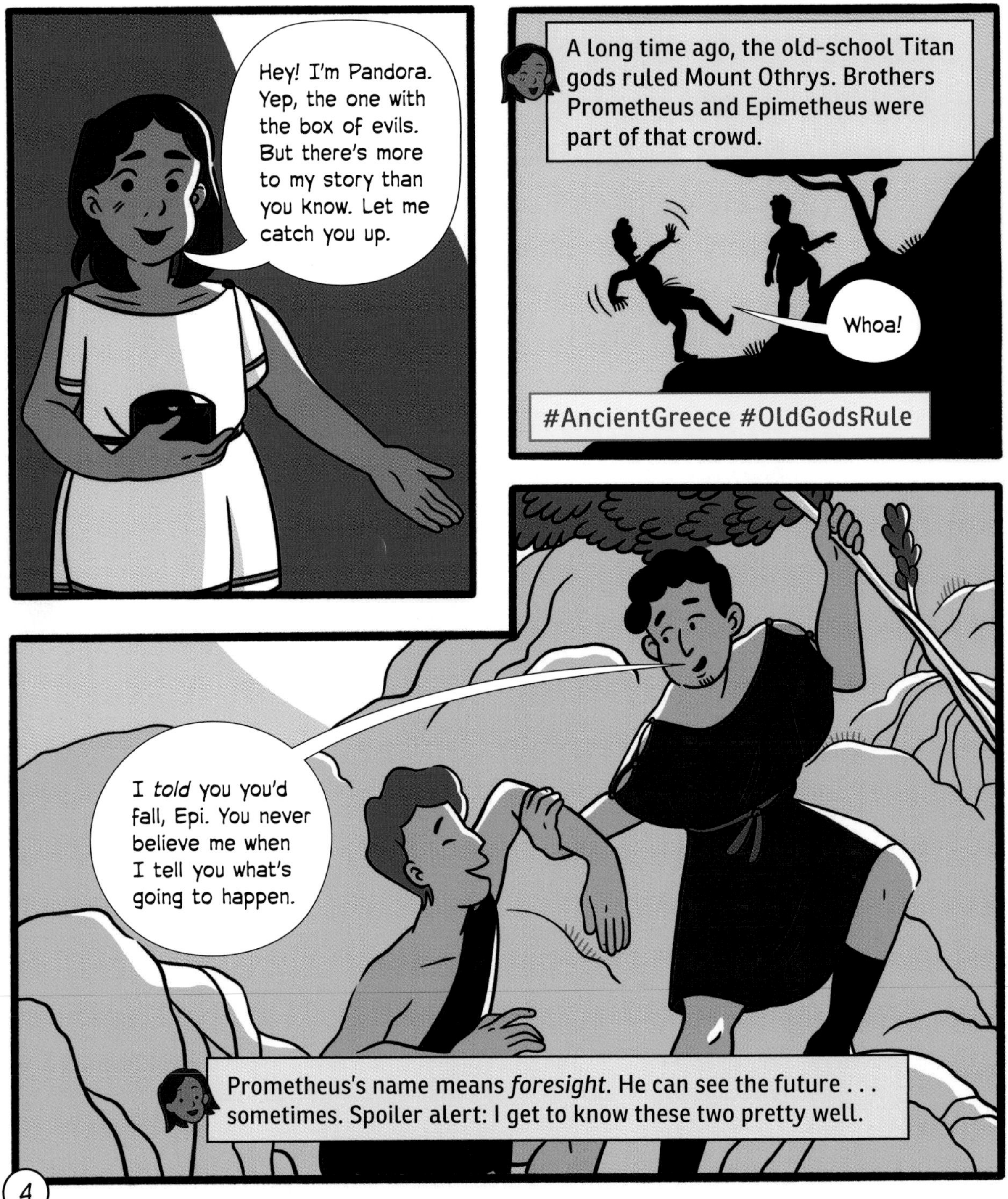
Hey! I'm Pandora. Yep, the one with the box of evils. But there's more to my story than you know. Let me catch you up.
A long time ago, the old-school Titan gods ruled Mount Othrys. Brothers Prometheus and Epimetheus were part of that crowd.
Whoa!
#AncientGreece #OldGodsRule
I *told* you you'd fall, Epi. You never believe me when I tell you what's going to happen.
Prometheus's name means *foresight*. He can see the future . . . sometimes. Spoiler alert: I get to know these two pretty well.

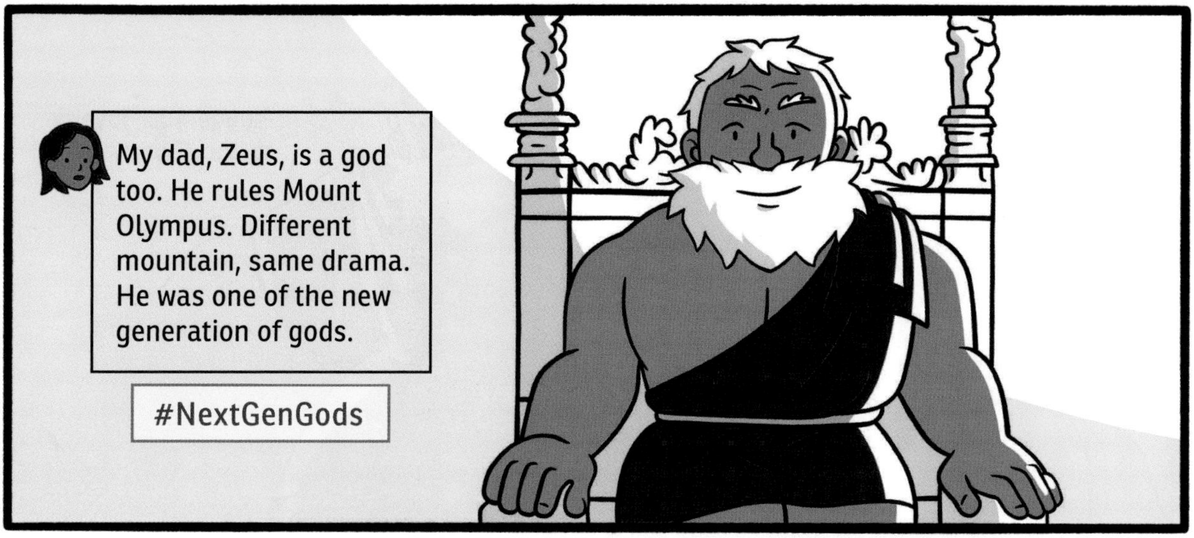
My dad, Zeus, is a god too. He rules Mount Olympus. Different mountain, same drama. He was one of the new generation of gods.
#NextGenGods

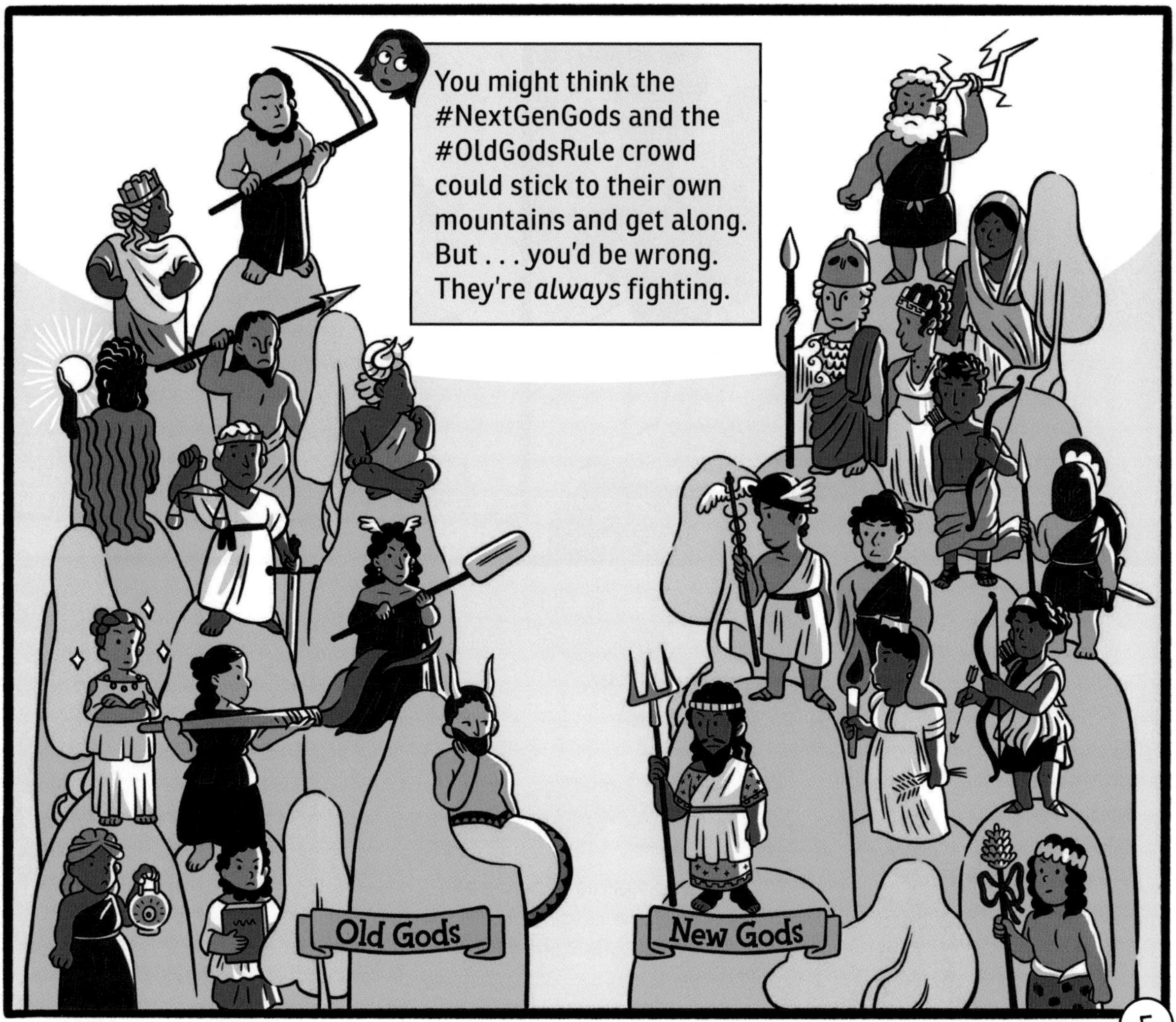
You might think the #NextGenGods and the #OldGodsRule crowd could stick to their own mountains and get along. But . . . you'd be wrong. They're *always* fighting.
Old Gods
New Gods

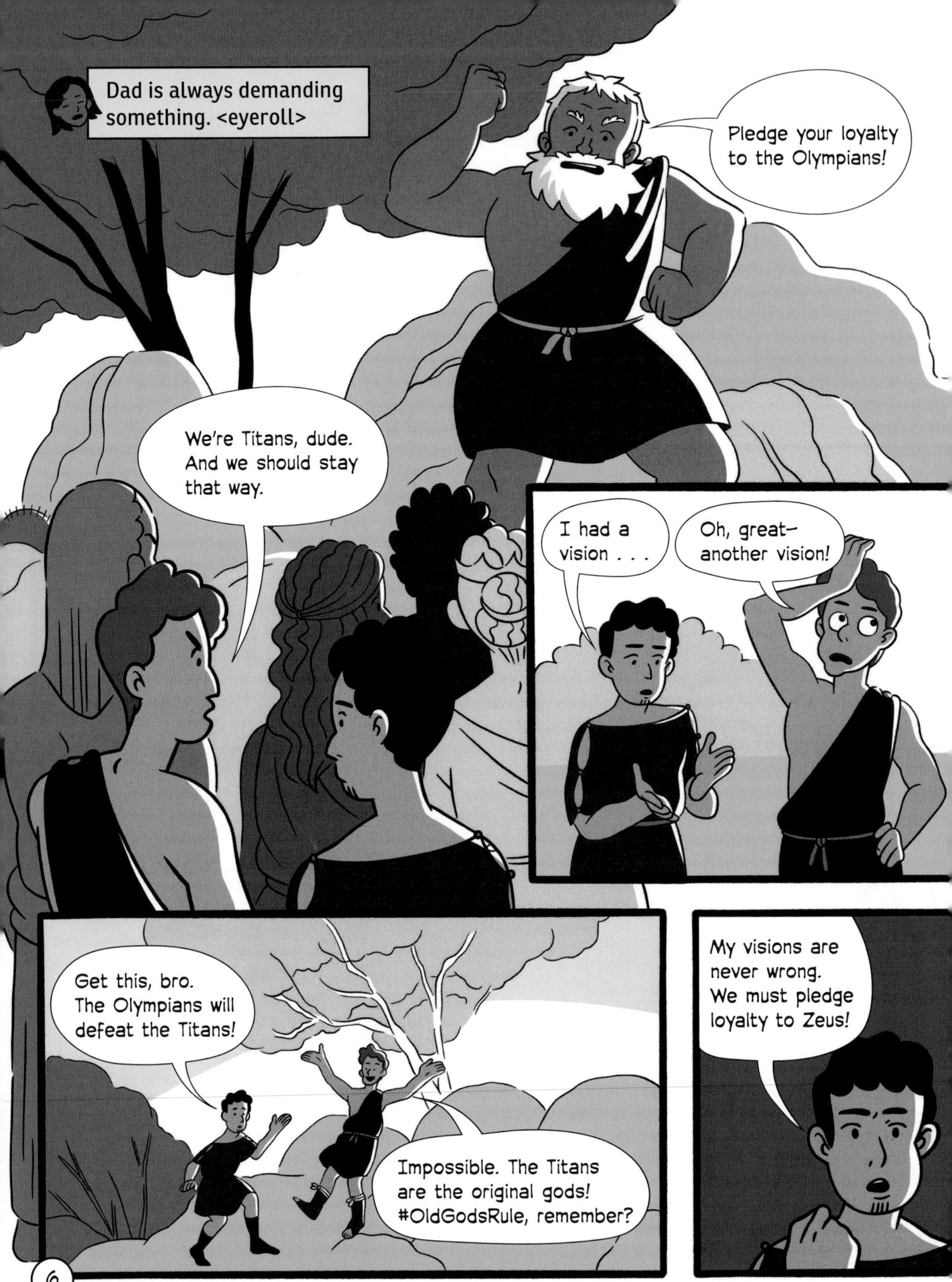
Dad is always demanding something. <eyeroll>
Pledge your loyalty to the Olympians!
We're Titans, dude. And we should stay that way.
I had a vision . . .
Oh, great—another vision!
Get this, bro. The Olympians will defeat the Titans!
Impossible. The Titans are the original gods! #OldGodsRule, remember?
My visions are never wrong. We must pledge loyalty to Zeus!

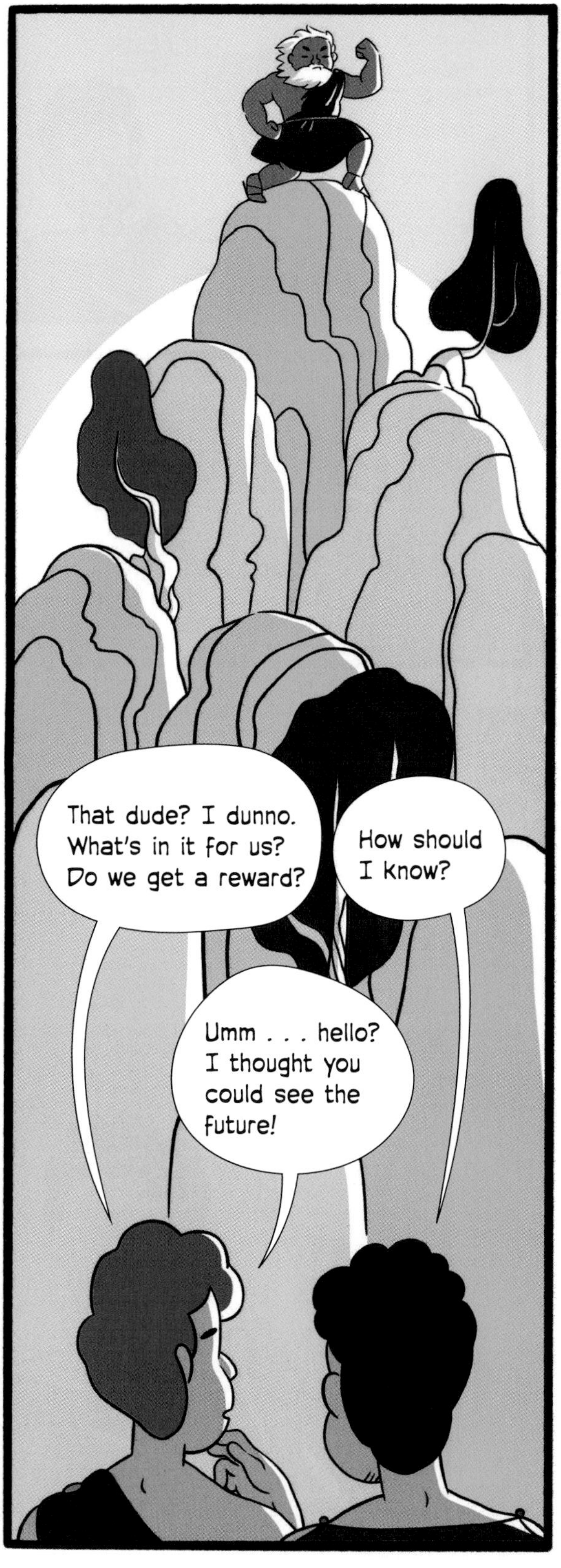
That dude? I dunno. What's in it for us? Do we get a reward?
How should I know?
Umm . . . hello? I thought you could see the future!

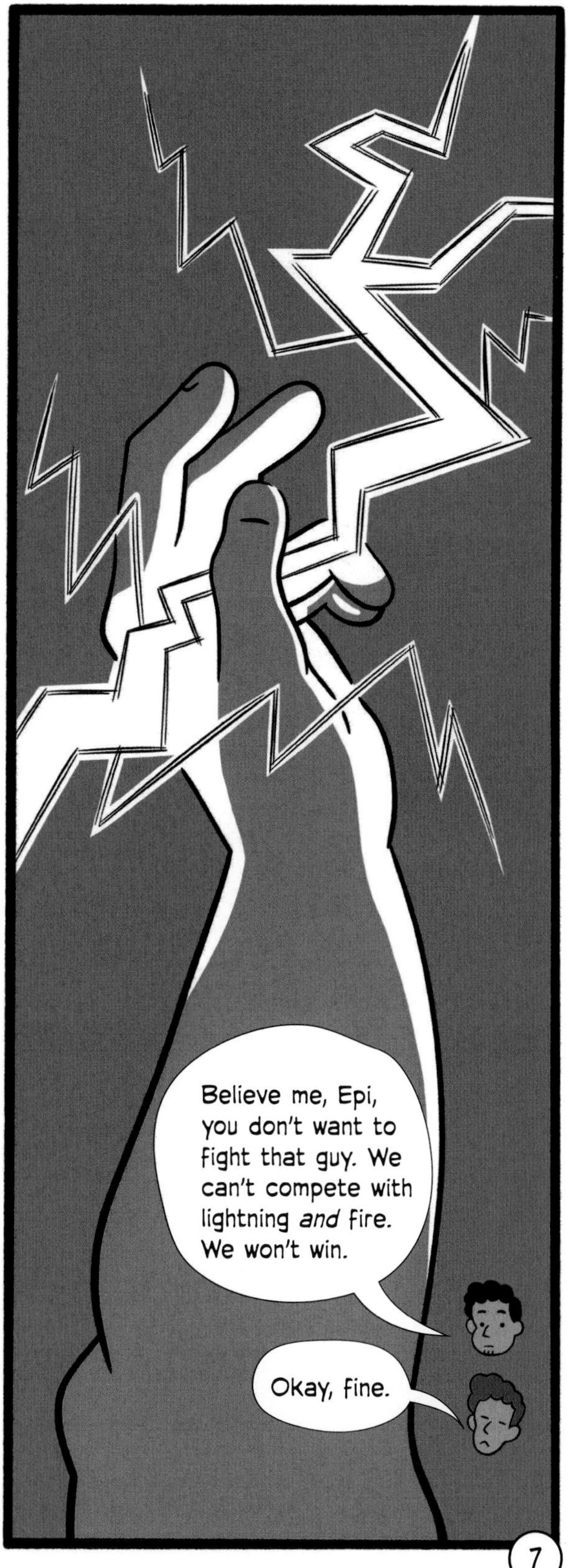
Believe me, Epi, you don't want to fight that guy. We can't compete with lightning *and* fire. We won't win.
Okay, fine.

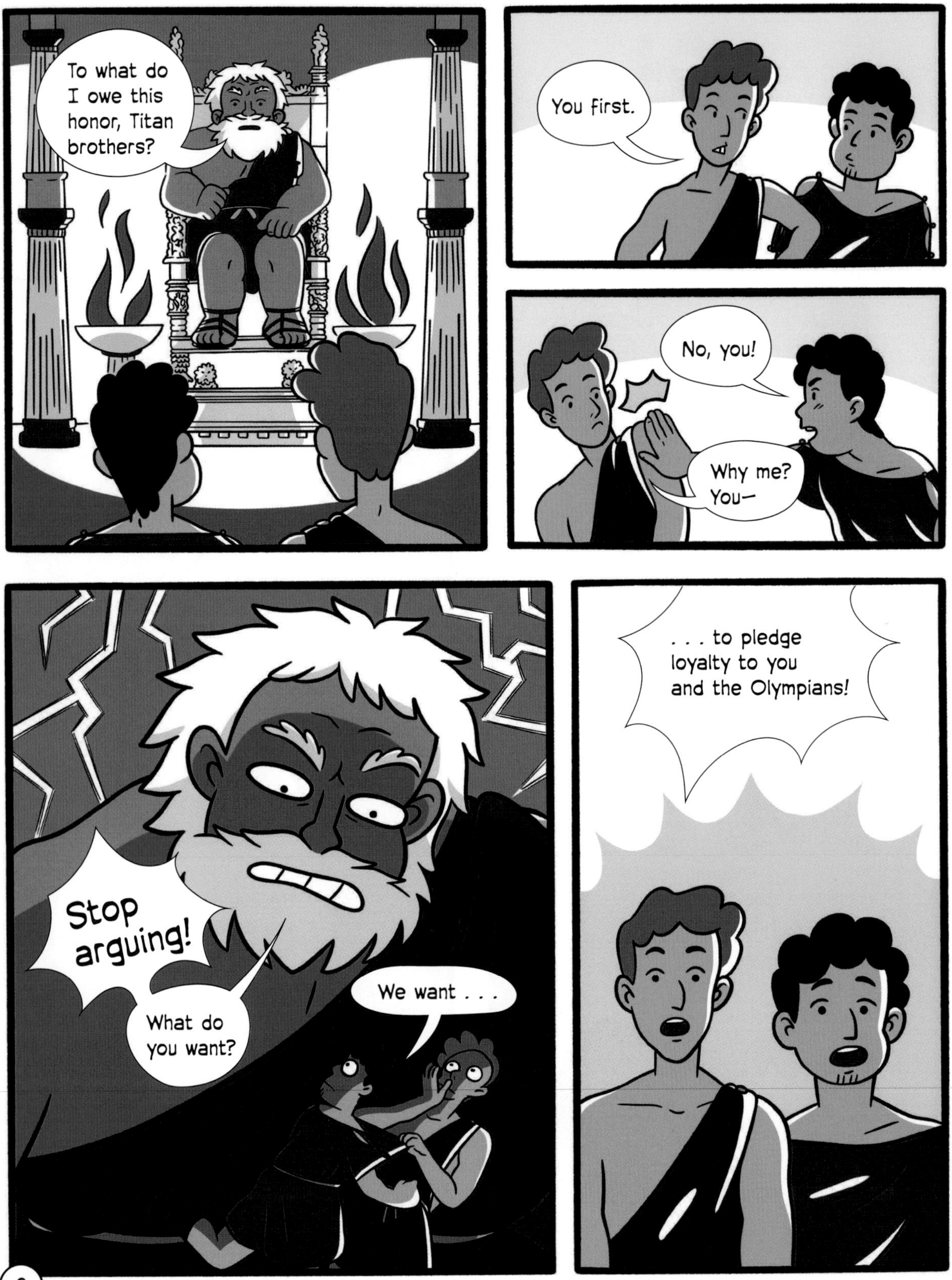
To what do I owe this honor, Titan brothers?
You first.
No, you!
Why me? You—
Stop arguing!
What do you want?
We want . . .
. . . to pledge loyalty to you and the Olympians!

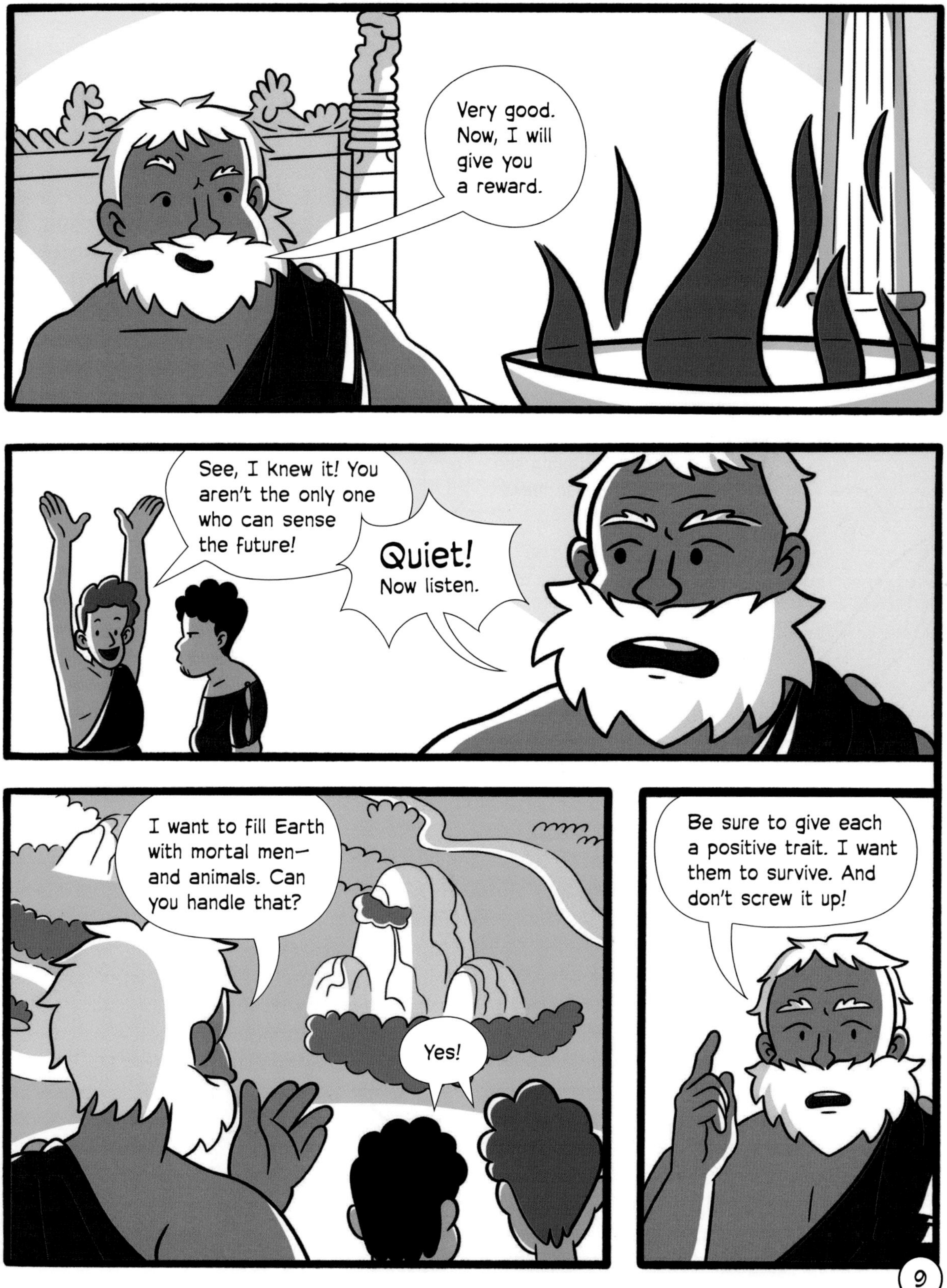
Very good. Now, I will give you a reward.
See, I knew it! You aren't the only one who can sense the future!
Quiet! Now listen.
I want to fill Earth with mortal men—and animals. Can you handle that?
Yes!
Be sure to give each a positive trait. I want them to survive. And don't screw it up!

CHAPTER 2

DIDN'T SEE THAT COMING!

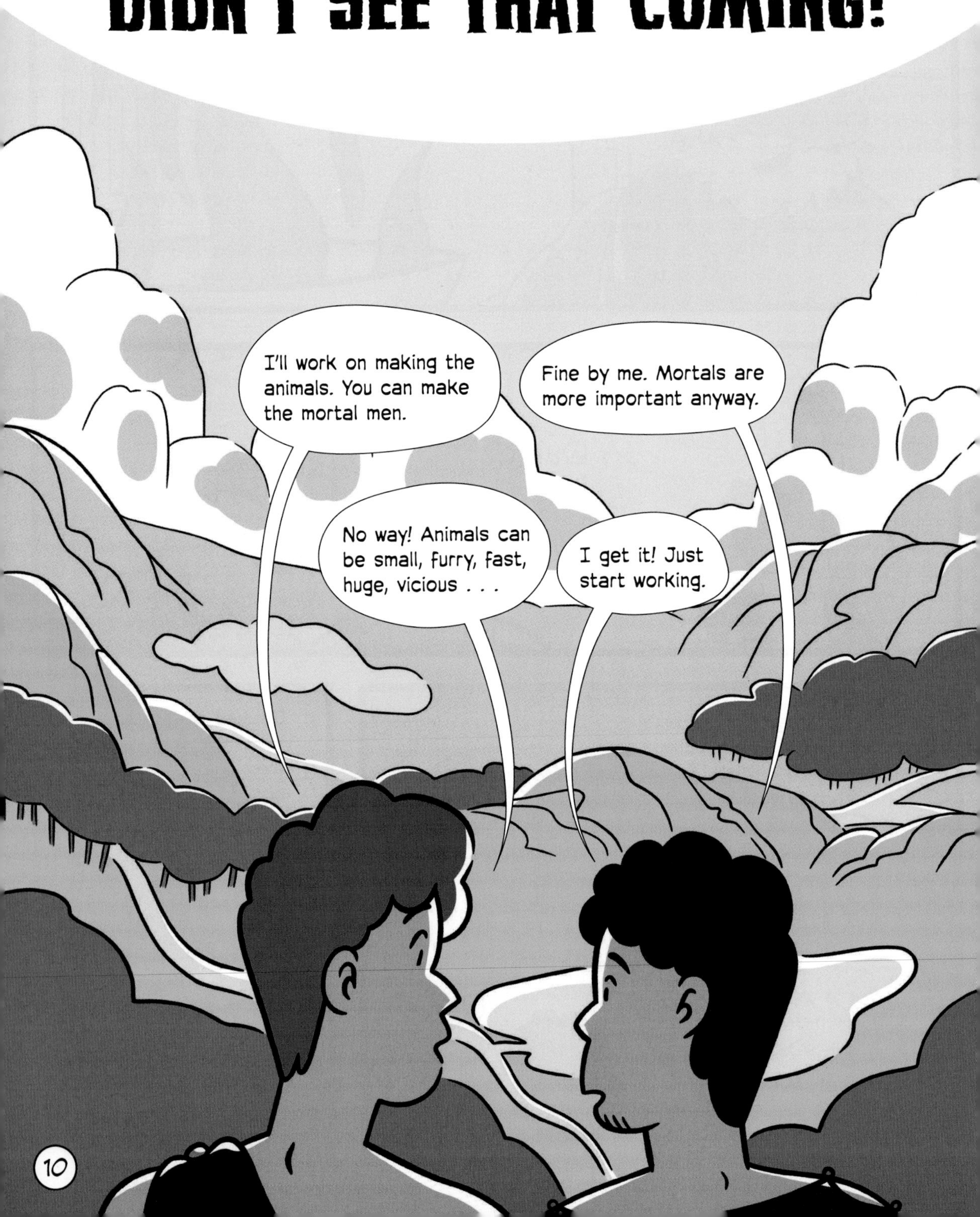

I'll work on making the animals. You can make the mortal men.
Fine by me. Mortals are more important anyway.
No way! Animals can be small, furry, fast, huge, vicious . . .
I get it! Just start working.

Prometheus goes off to create mortal men. Epimetheus gets to work on the animals. He makes them in all different shapes and sizes.

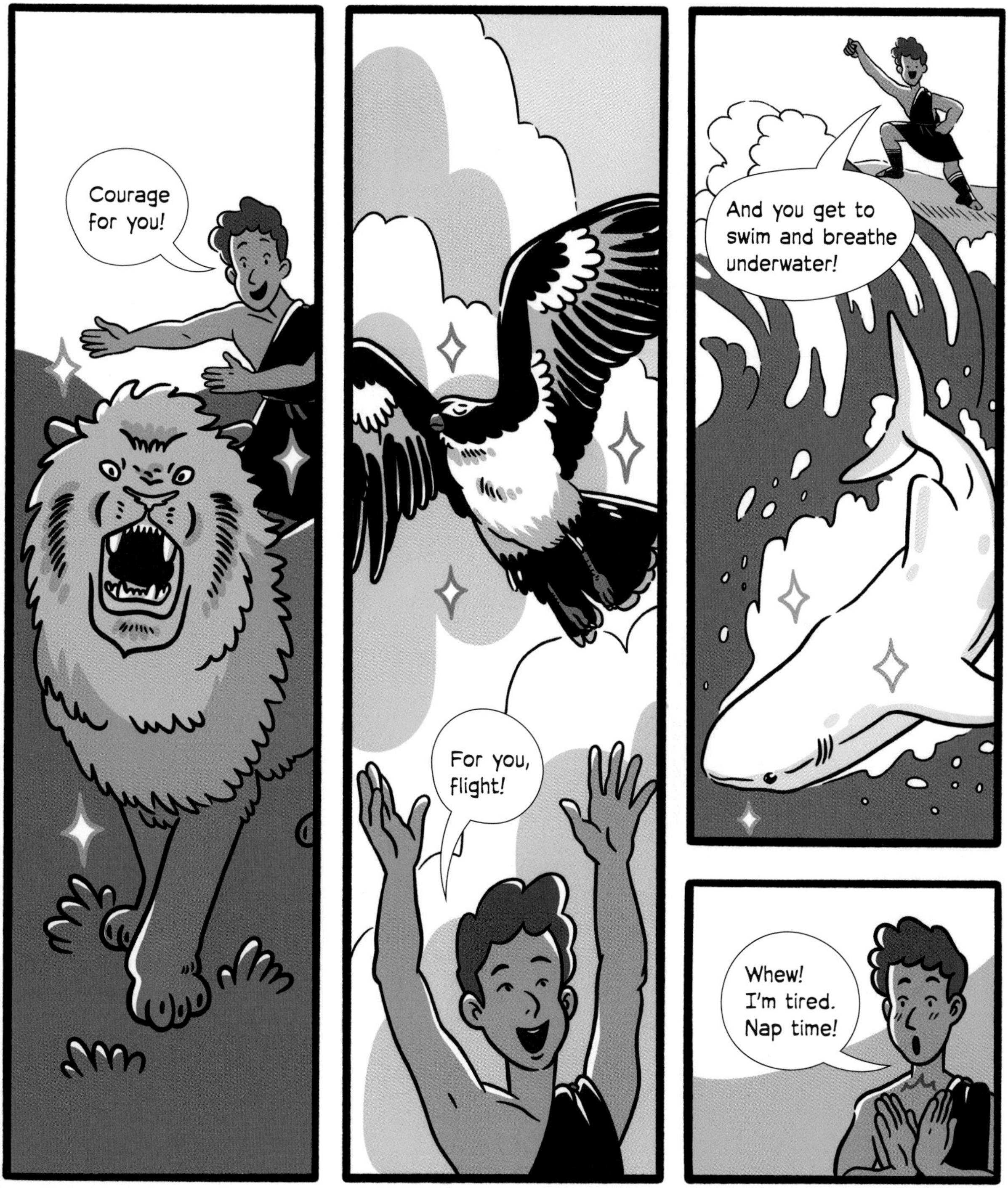
Courage for you!
For you, flight!
And you get to swim and breathe underwater!
Whew! I'm tired. Nap time!

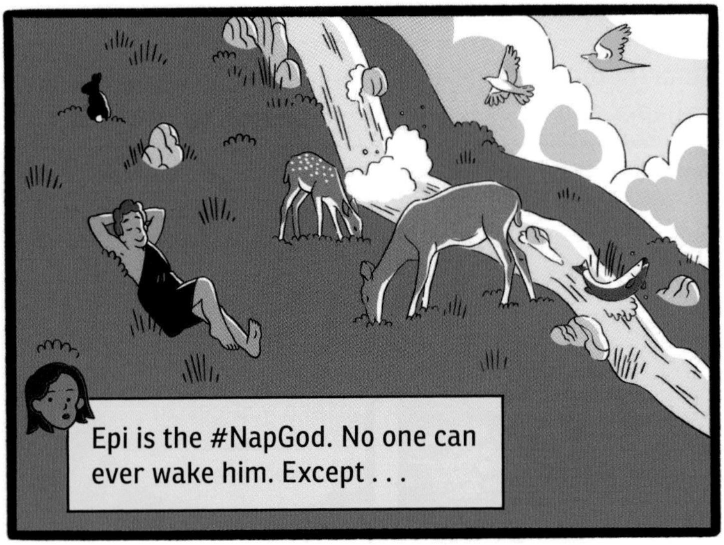
Epi is the #NapGod. No one can ever wake him. Except . . .

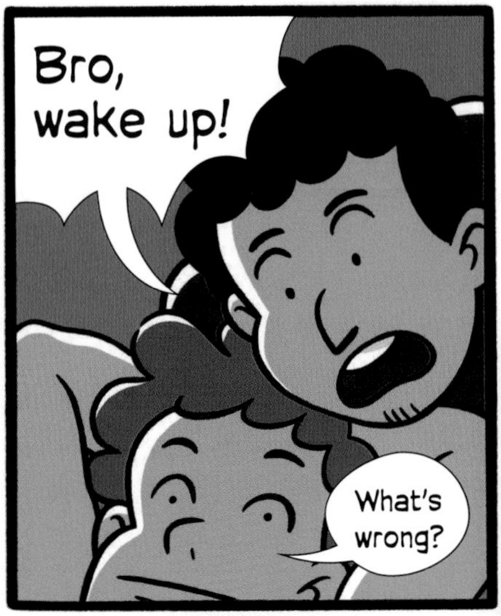
Bro, wake up!
What's wrong?

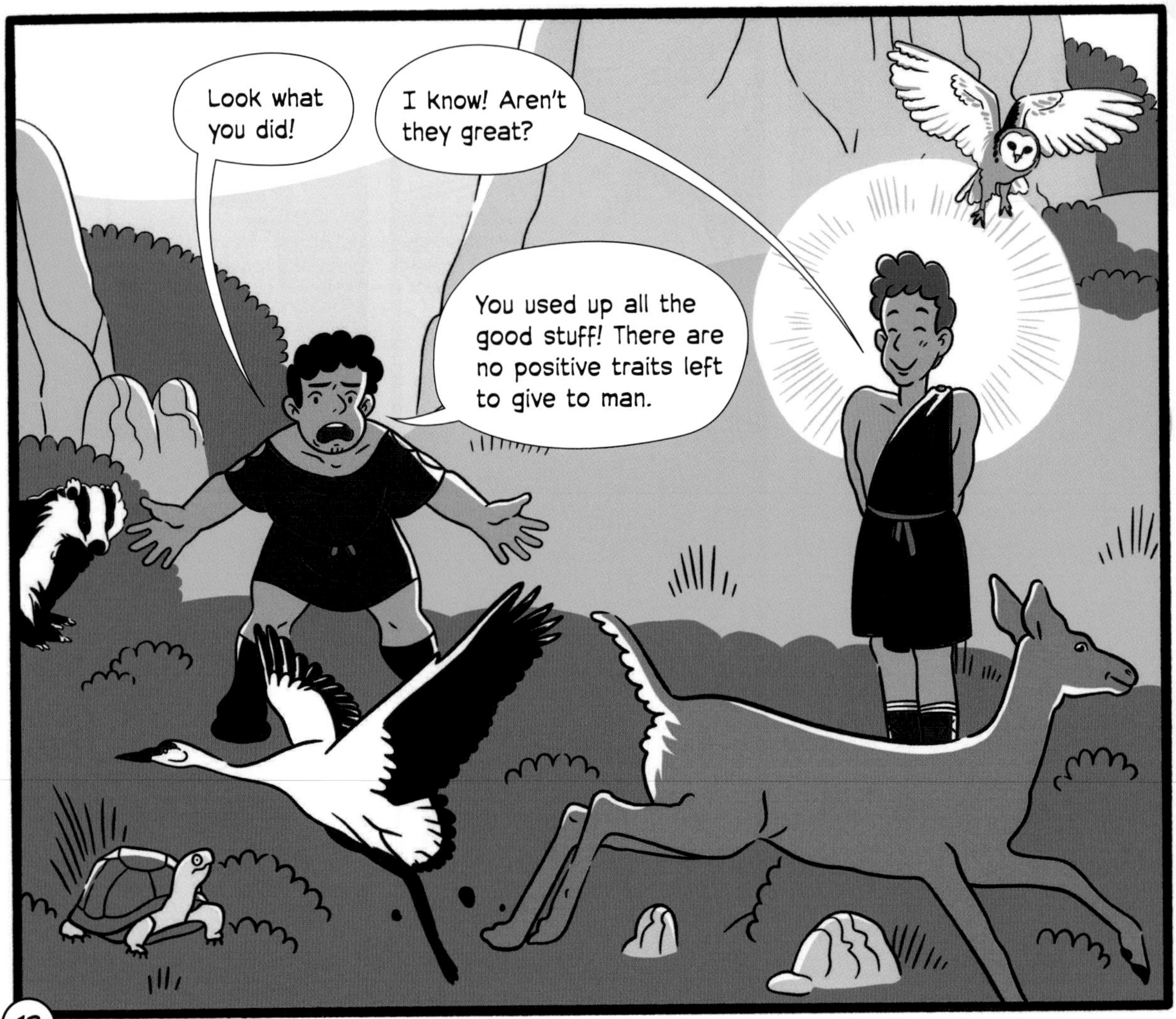
Look what you did!
I know! Aren't they great?
You used up all the good stuff! There are no positive traits left to give to man.

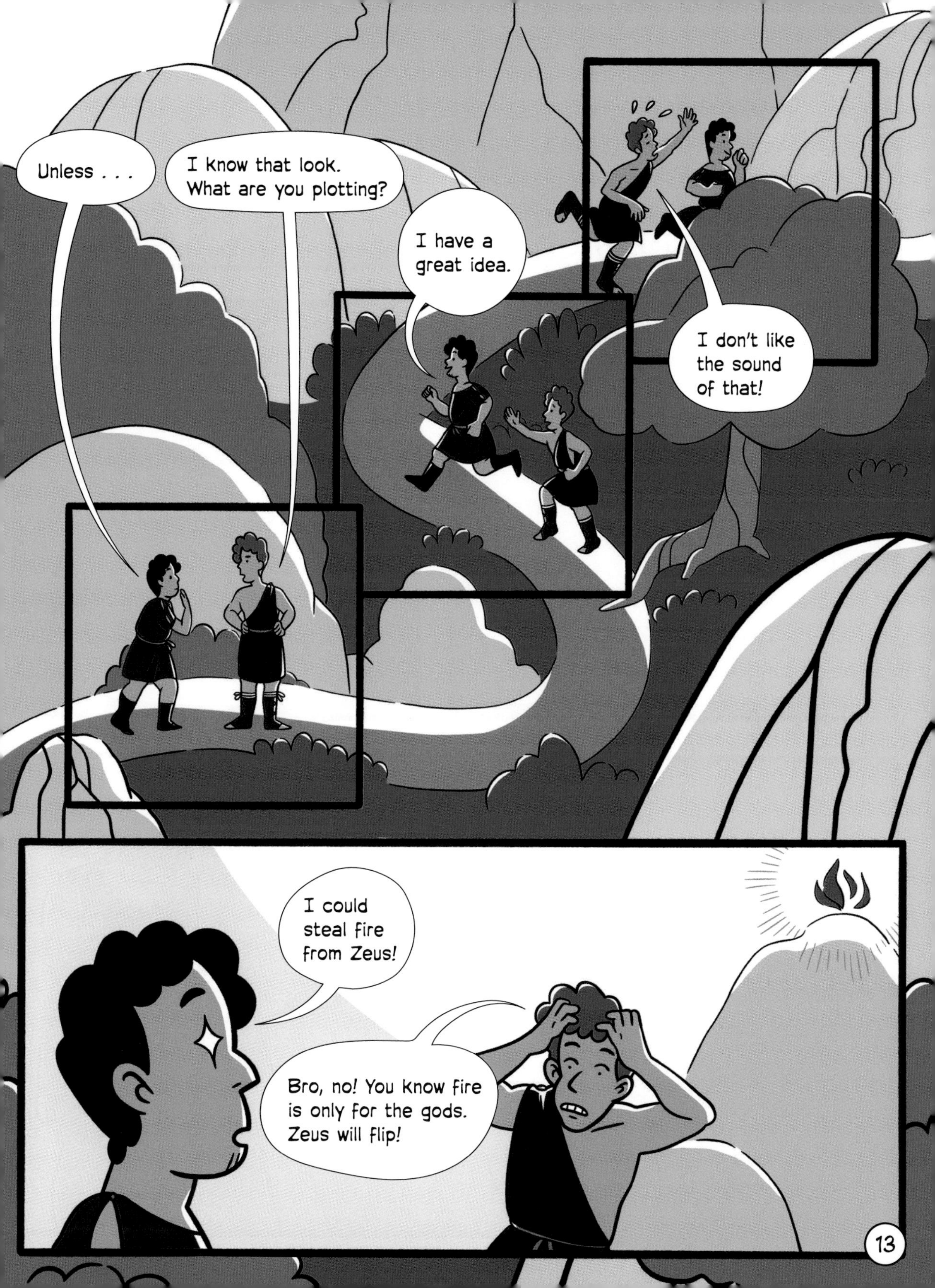
Unless . . .
I know that look. What are you plotting?
I have a great idea.
I don't like the sound of that!
I could steal fire from Zeus!
Bro, no! You know fire is only for the gods. Zeus will flip!

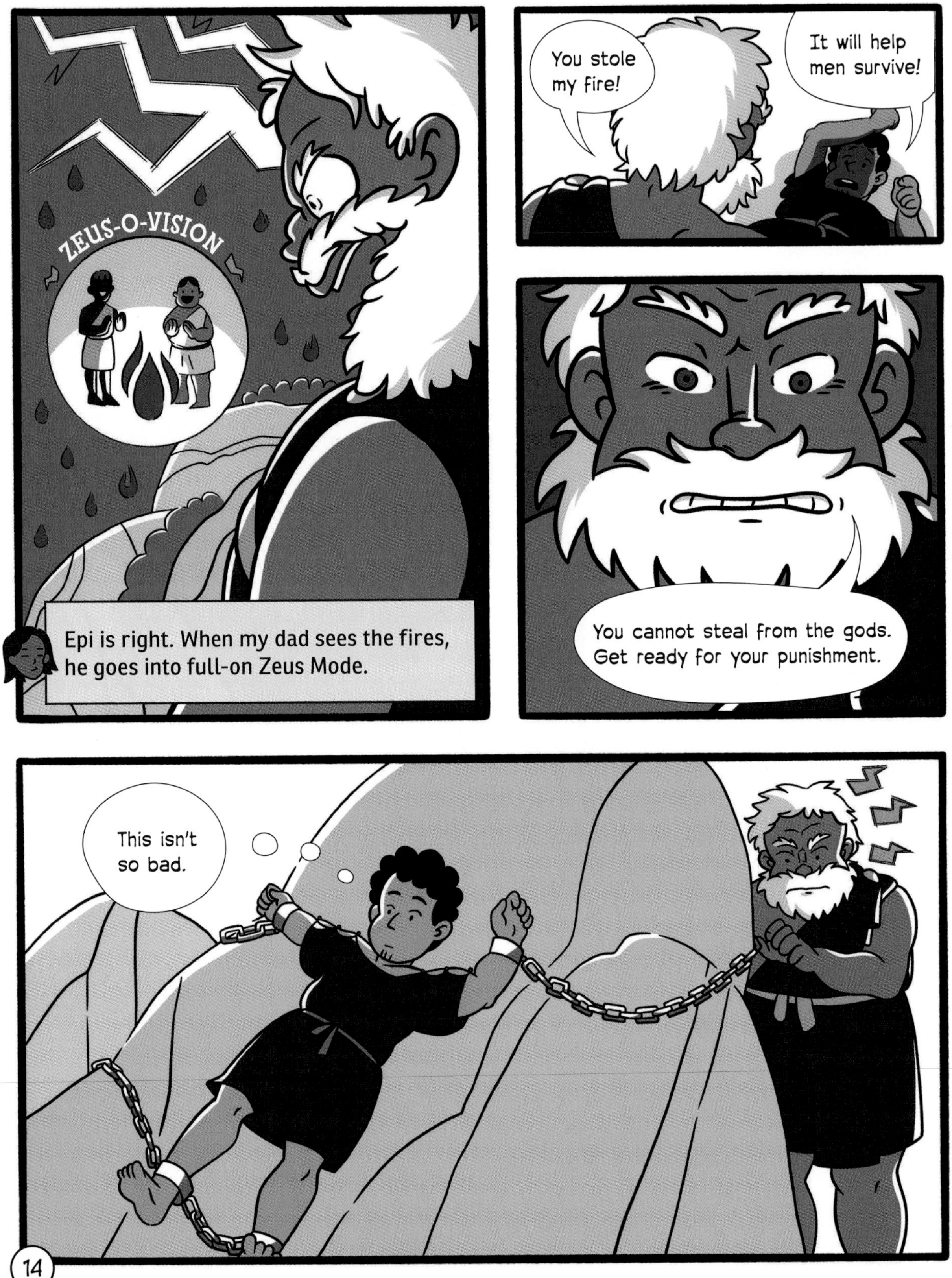
ZEUS-O-VISION
Epi is right. When my dad sees the fires, he goes into full-on Zeus Mode.
You stole my fire!
It will help men survive!
You cannot steal from the gods. Get ready for your punishment.
This isn't so bad.

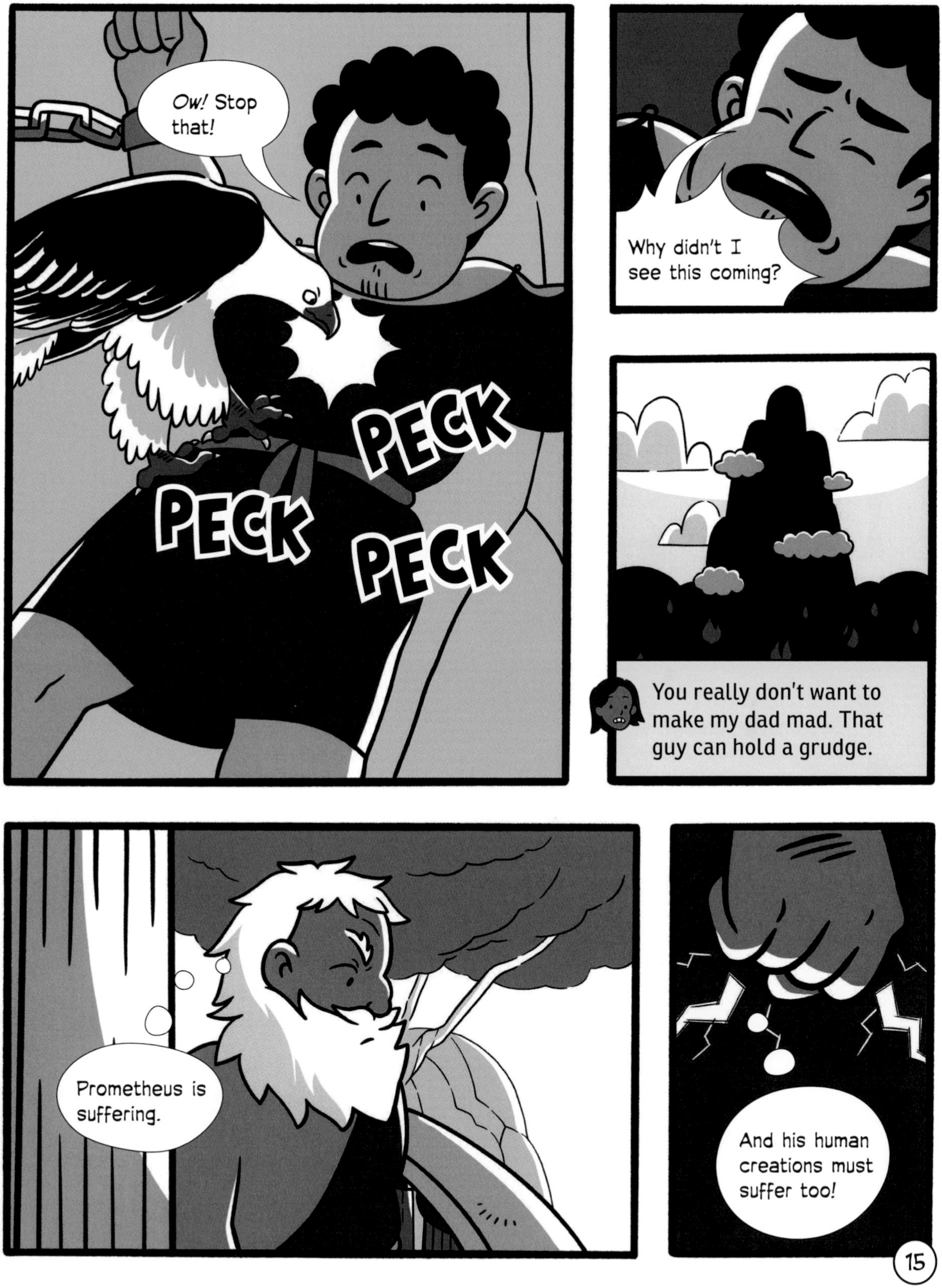

Ow! Stop that!
PECK
PECK
PECK
Why didn't I see this coming?
You really don't want to make my dad mad. That guy can hold a grudge.
Prometheus is suffering.
And his human creations must suffer too!

CHAPTER 3

SELFIE TIME!

You're probably wondering where I fit into this. Well, my dad decides to create his *own* mortal—me!

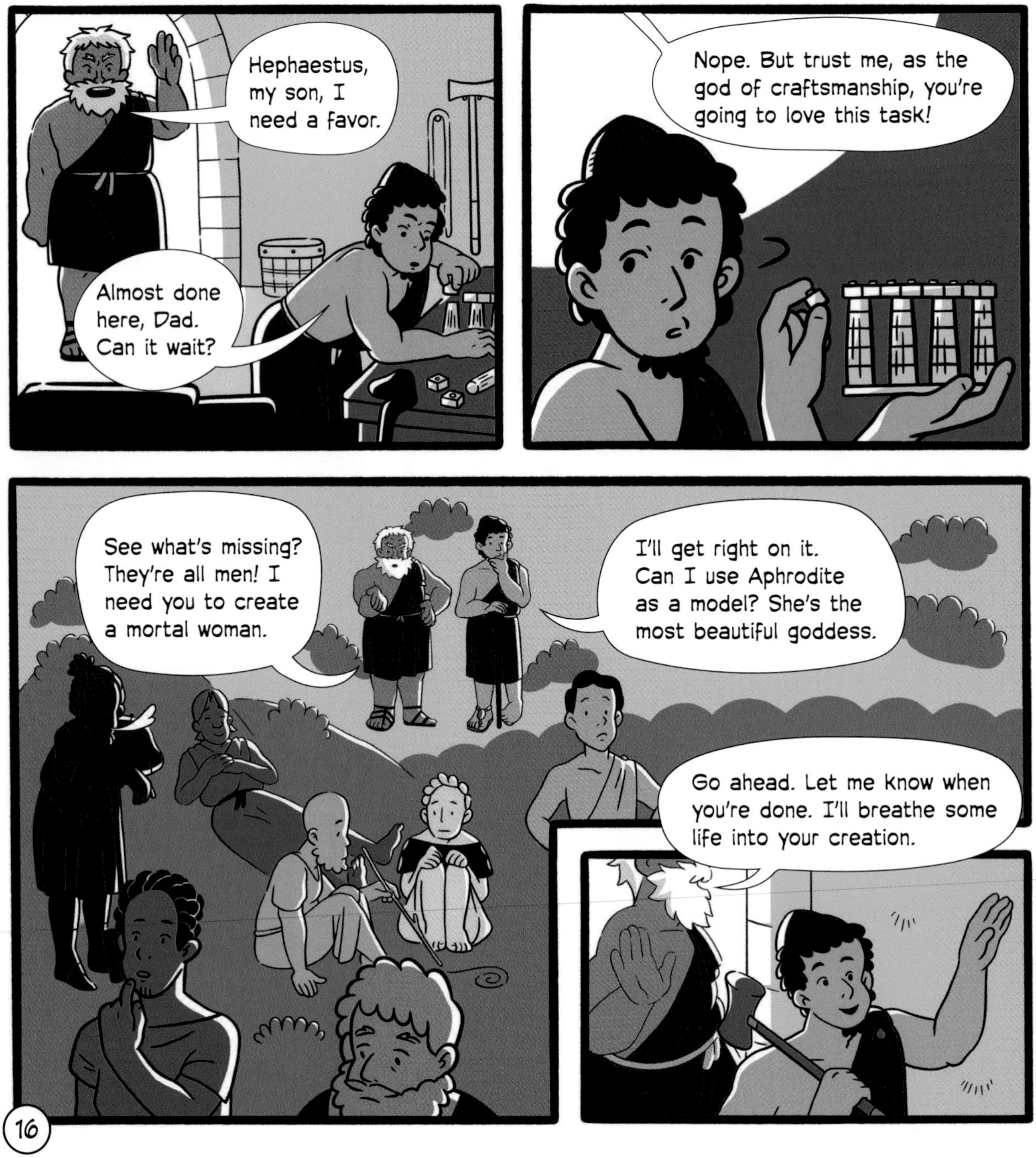
Hephaestus, my son, I need a favor.
Almost done here, Dad. Can it wait?
Nope. But trust me, as the god of craftsmanship, you're going to love this task!
See what's missing? They're all men! I need you to create a mortal woman.
I'll get right on it. Can I use Aphrodite as a model? She's the most beautiful goddess.
Go ahead. Let me know when you're done. I'll breathe some life into your creation.

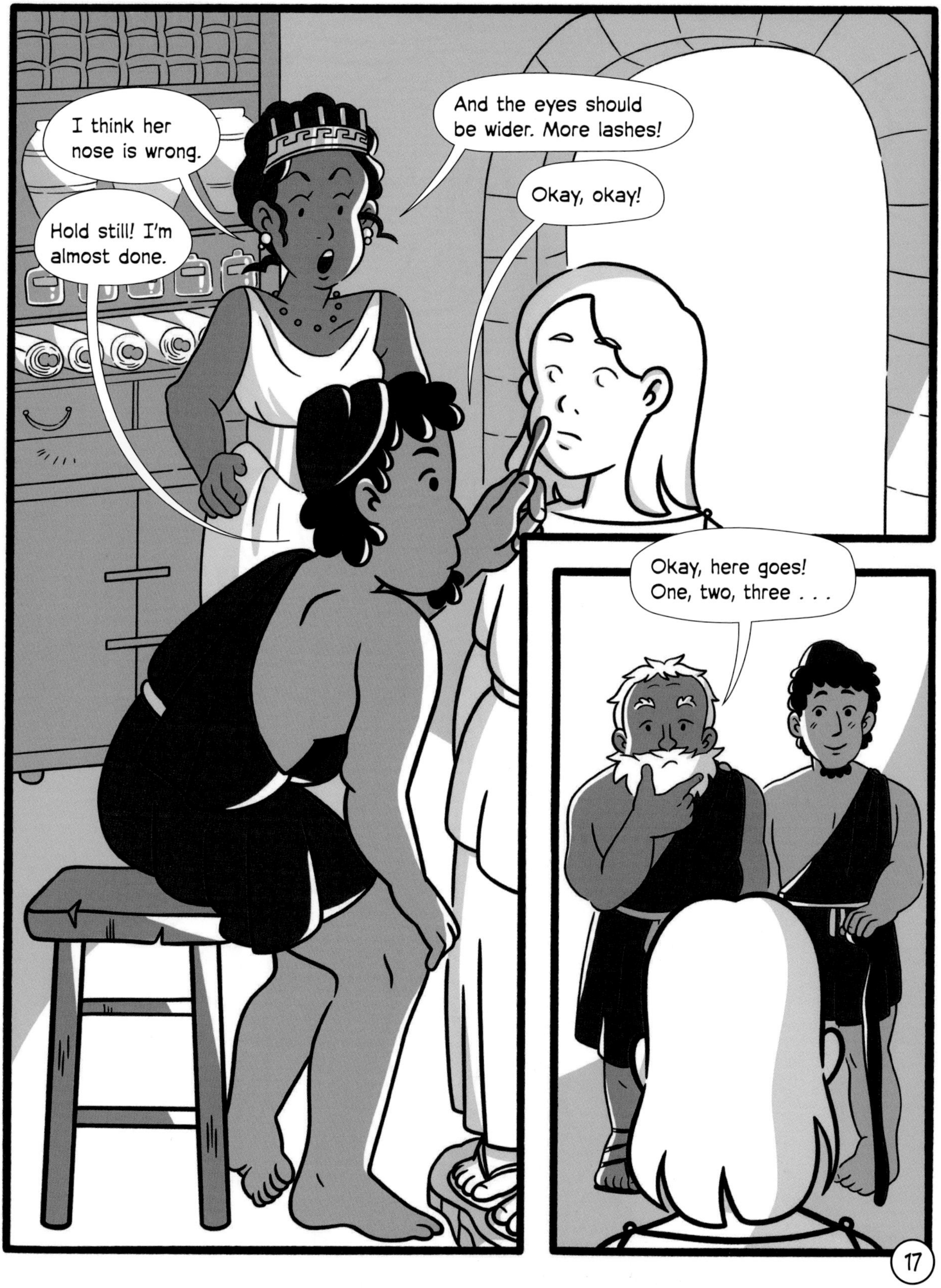
I think her nose is wrong.
And the eyes should be wider. More lashes!
Hold still! I'm almost done.
Okay, okay!
Okay, here goes! One, two, three . . .

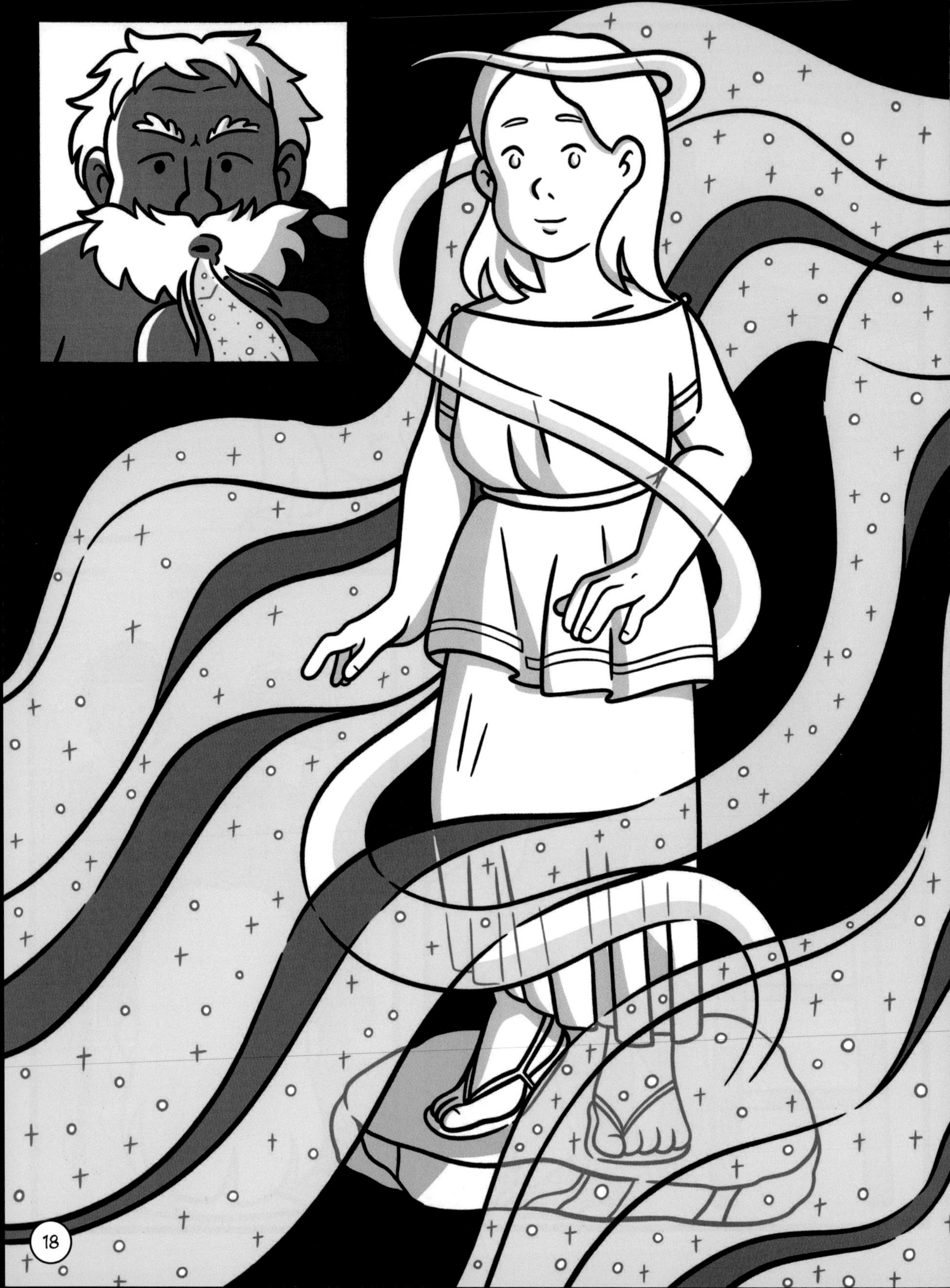

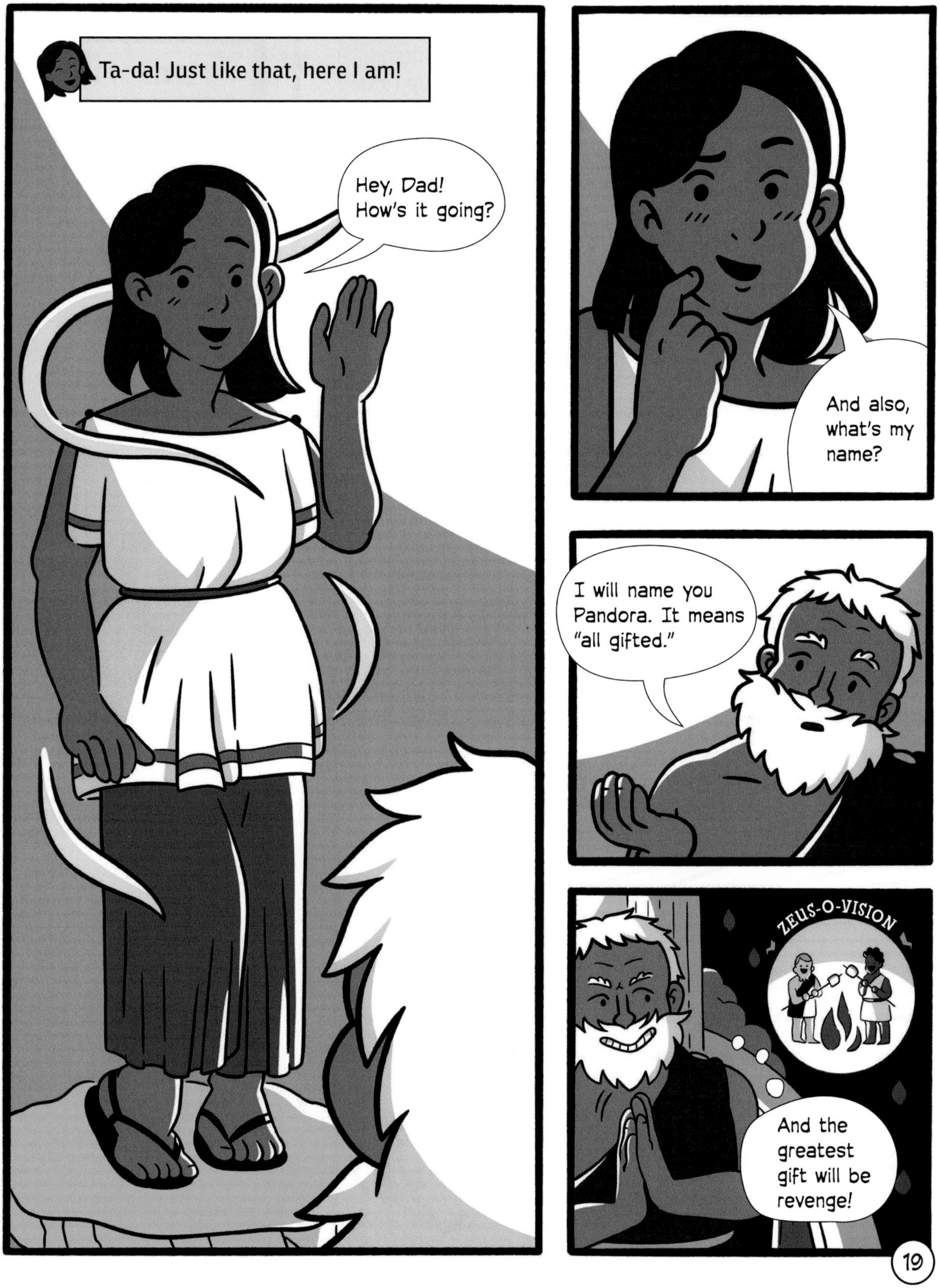
Ta-da! Just like that, here I am!
Hey, Dad! How's it going?
And also, what's my name?
I will name you Pandora. It means "all gifted."
ZEUS-O-VISION
And the greatest gift will be revenge!

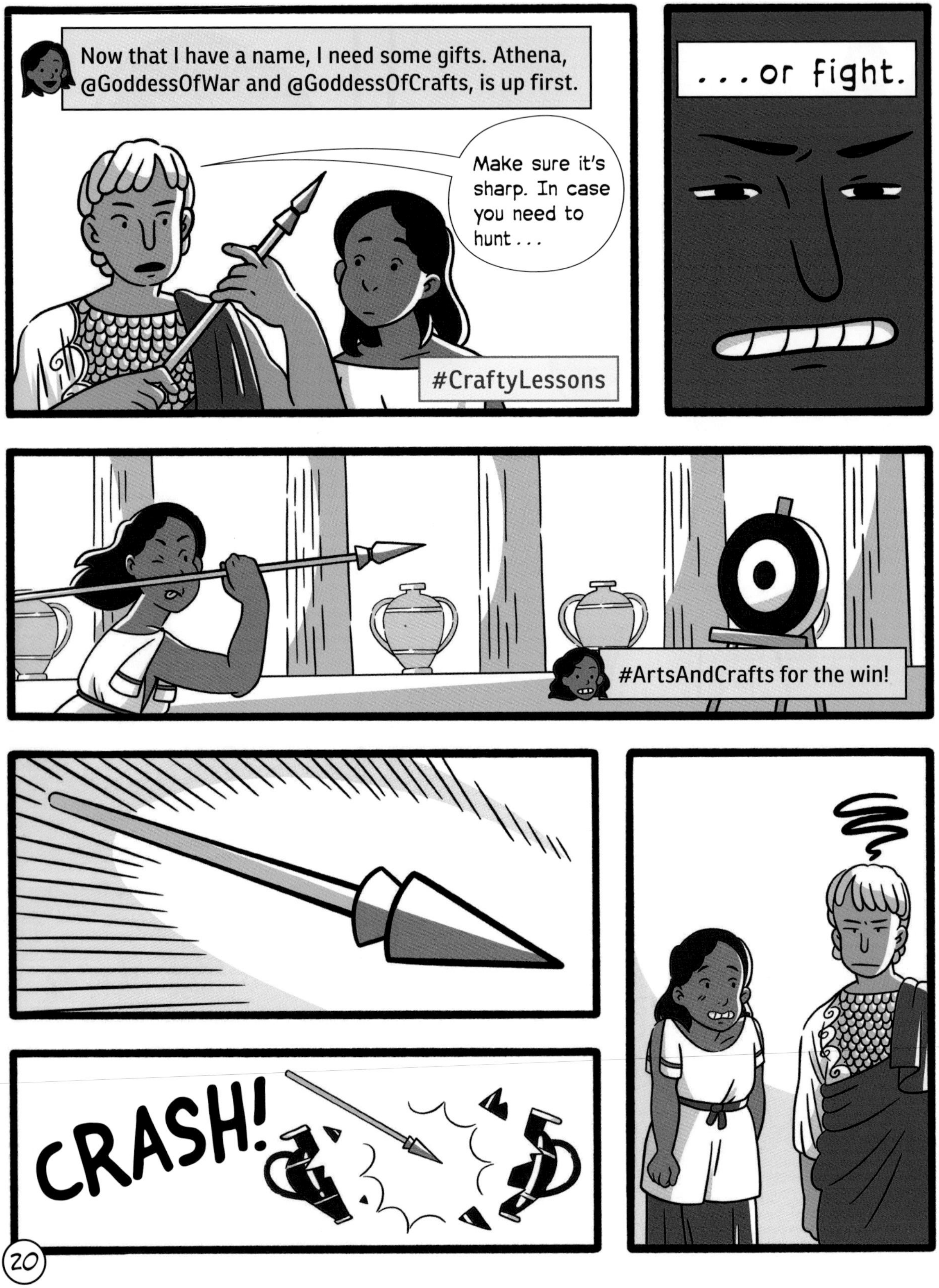

Now that I have a name, I need some gifts. Athena, @GoddessOfWar and @GoddessOfCrafts, is up first.
Make sure it's sharp. In case you need to hunt . . .
#CraftyLessons
. . . or fight.
#ArtsAndCrafts for the win!
CRASH!

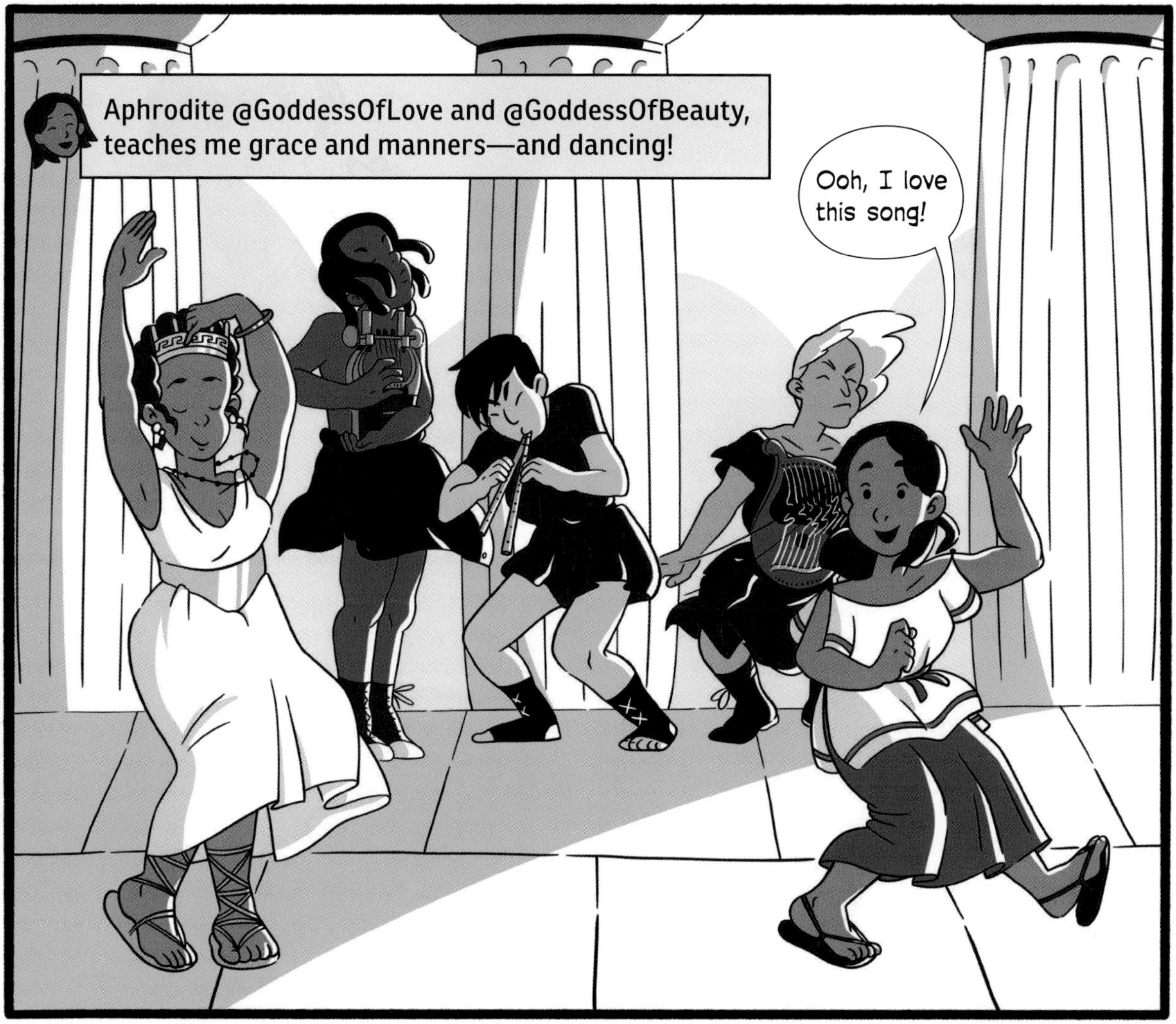
Aphrodite @GoddessOfLove and @GoddessOfBeauty, teaches me grace and manners—and dancing!
Ooh, I love this song!

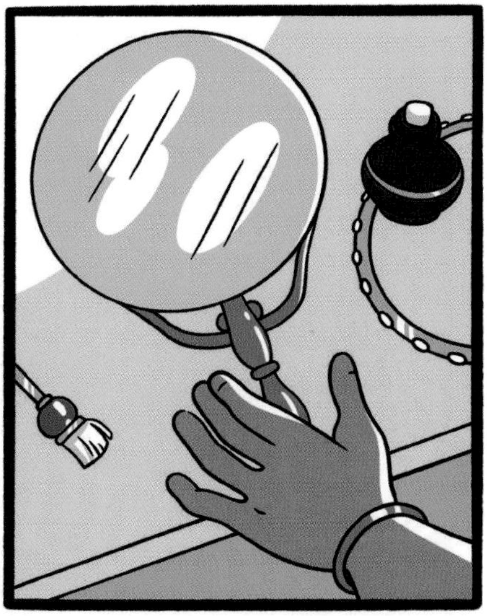

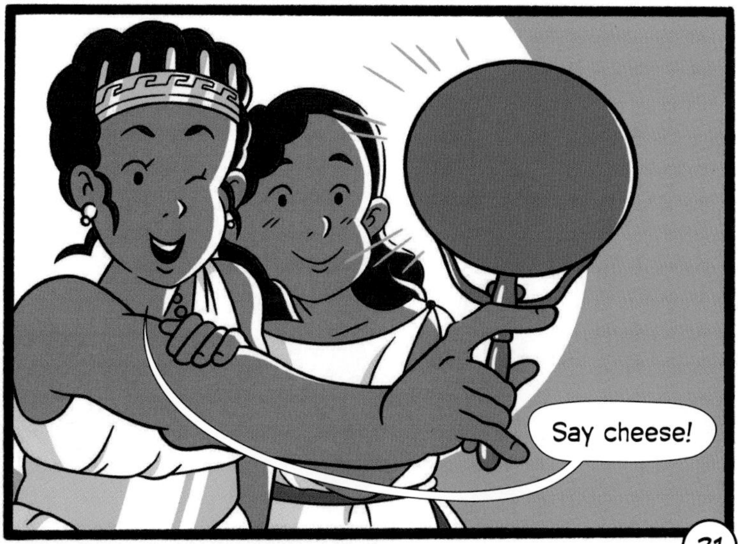
Say cheese!

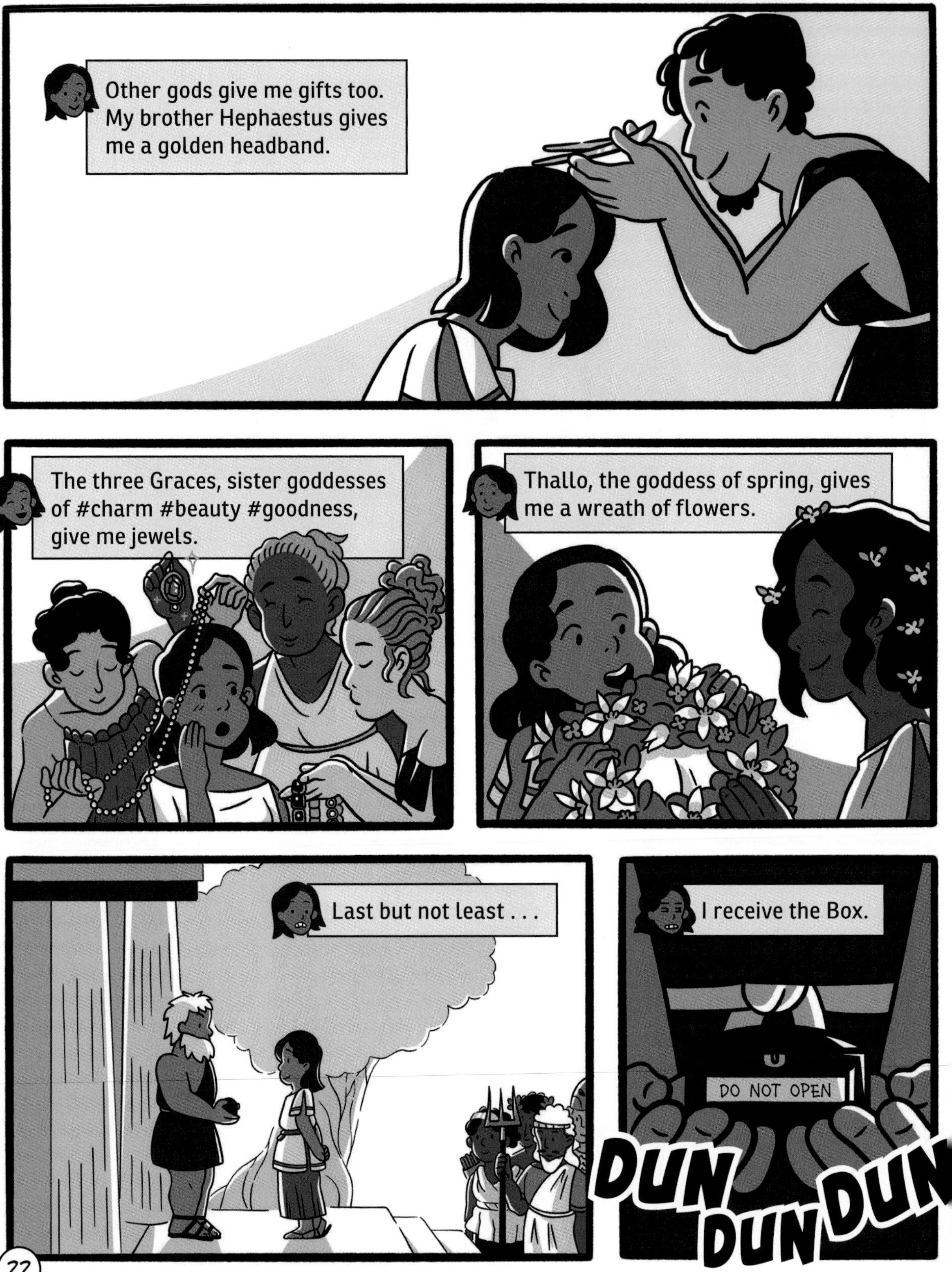
Other gods give me gifts too. My brother Hephaestus gives me a golden headband.
The three Graces, sister goddesses of #charm #beauty #goodness, give me jewels.
Thallo, the goddess of spring, gives me a wreath of flowers.
Last but not least . . .
I receive the Box.
DO NOT OPEN
DUN DUN DUN

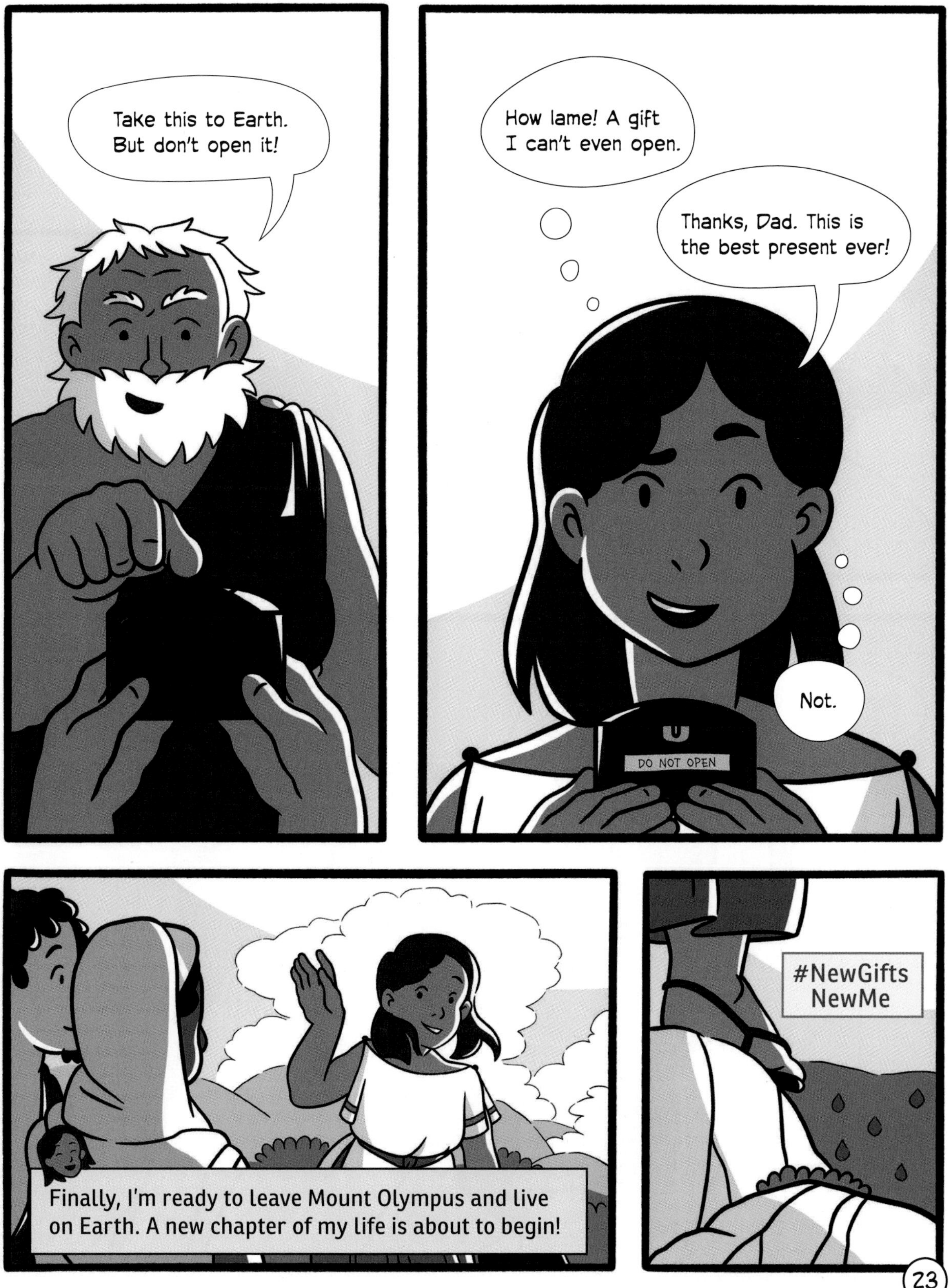
Take this to Earth. But don't open it!
How lame! A gift I can't even open.
Thanks, Dad. This is the best present ever!
Not.
DO NOT OPEN
Finally, I'm ready to leave Mount Olympus and live on Earth. A new chapter of my life is about to begin!
#NewGifts NewMe

CHAPTER 4

#LoveAtFirstSight

Meanwhile, the #TitanBrothers have *not* been having a great time . . .

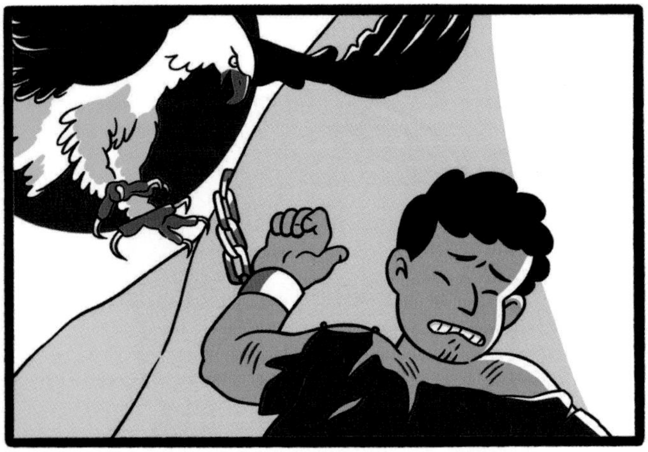

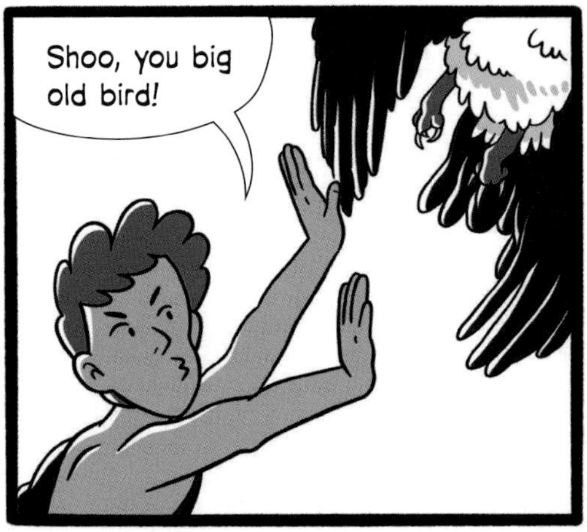
Shoo, you big old bird!

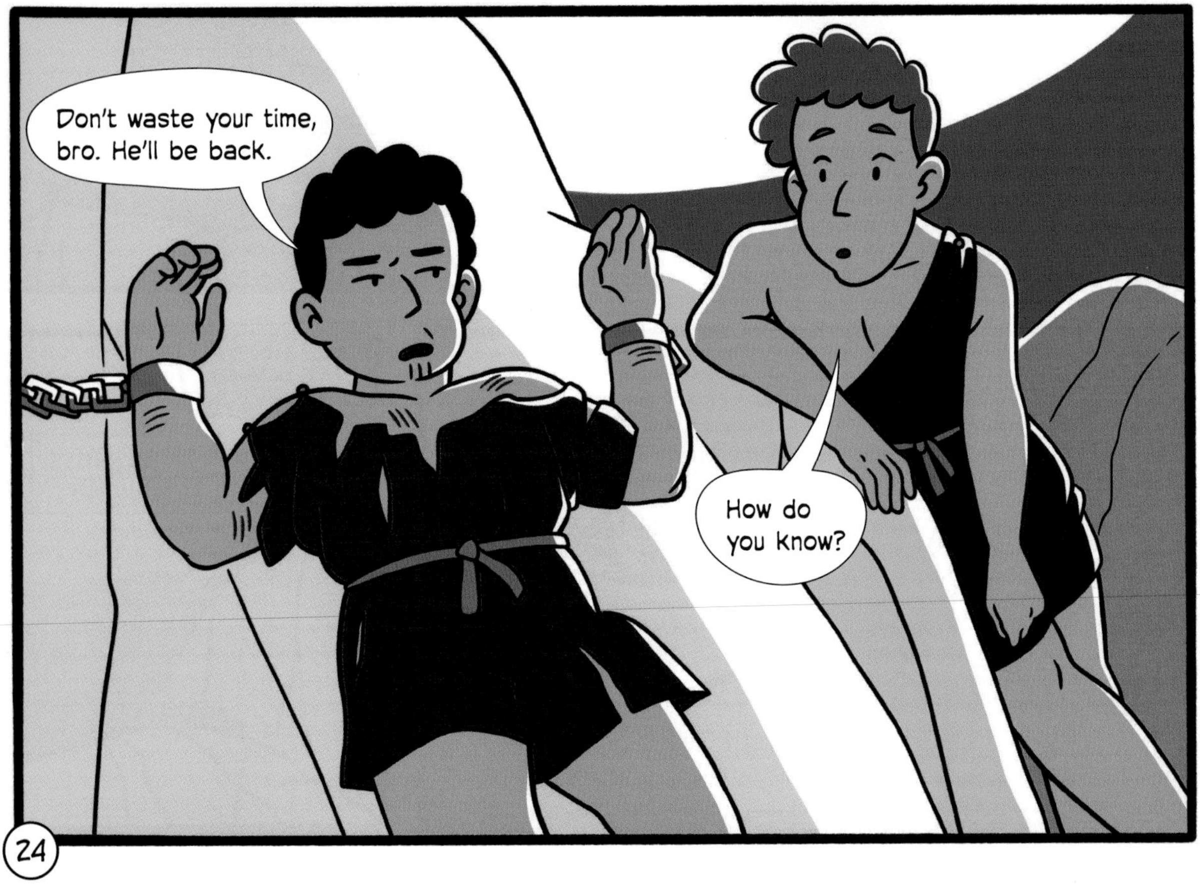
Don't waste your time, bro. He'll be back.
How do you know?

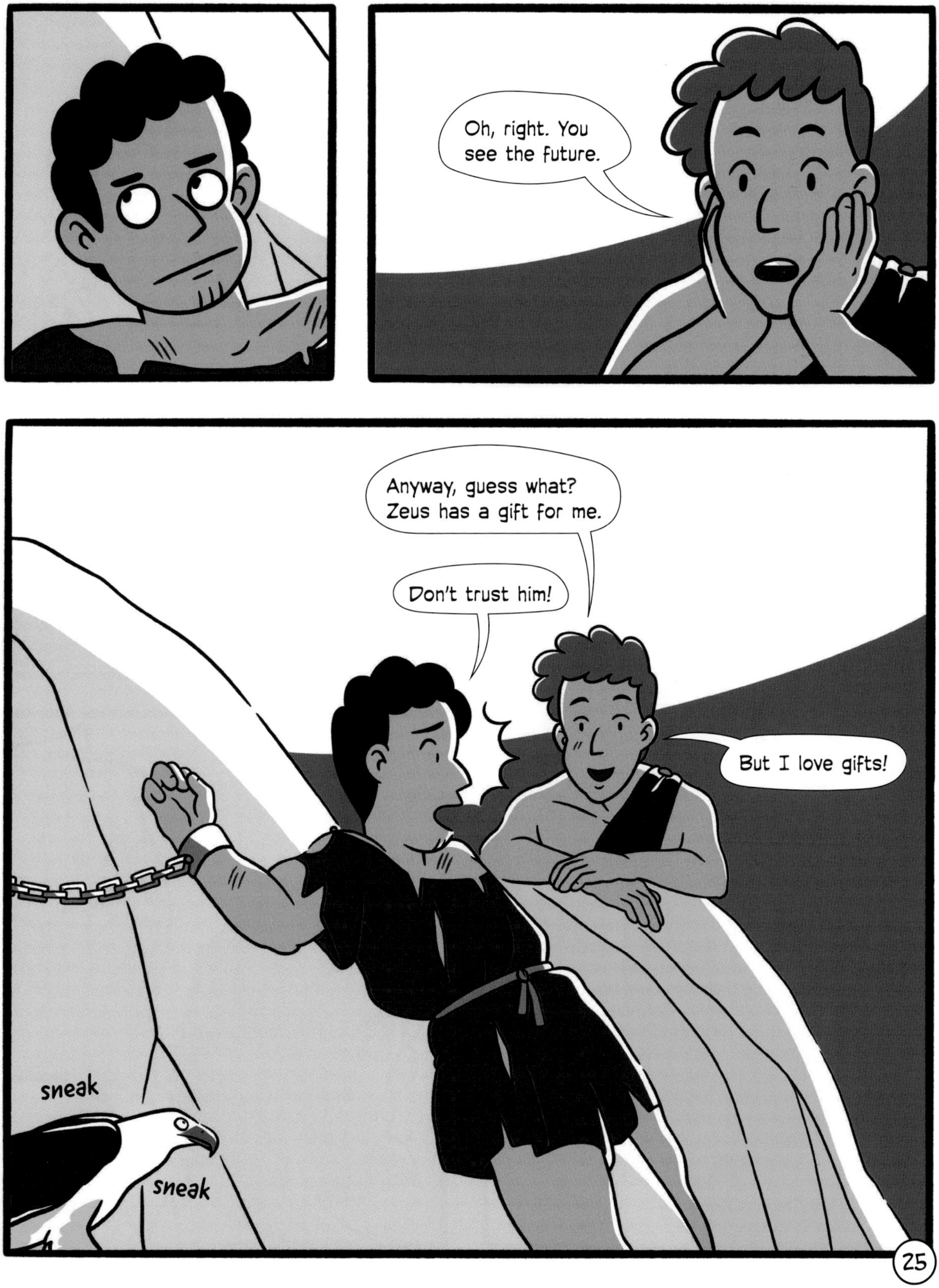
Oh, right. You see the future.
Anyway, guess what? Zeus has a gift for me.
Don't trust him!
But I love gifts!
sneak
sneak

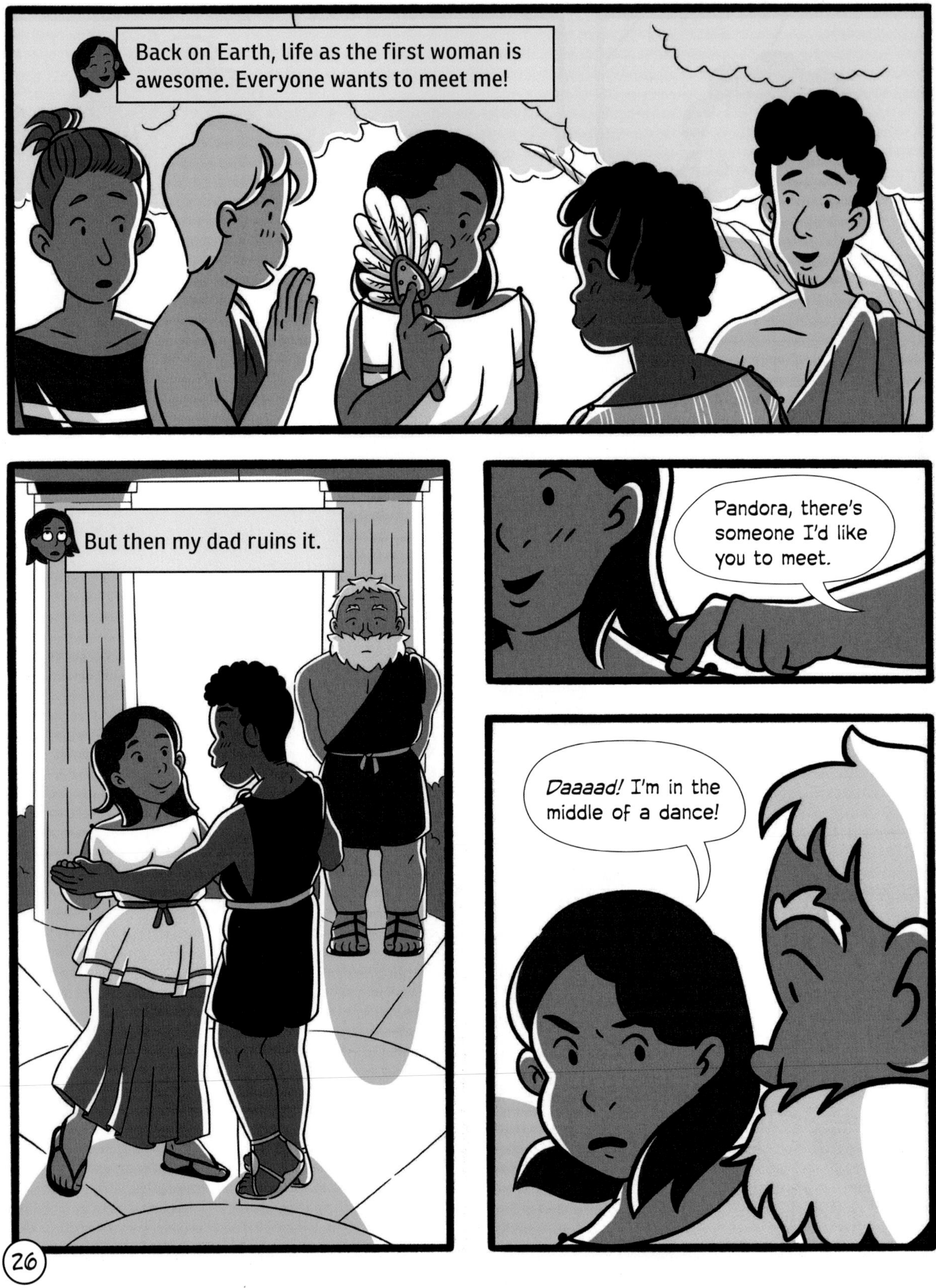
Back on Earth, life as the first woman is awesome. Everyone wants to meet me!
But then my dad ruins it.
Pandora, there's someone I'd like you to meet.
Daaaad! I'm in the middle of a dance!

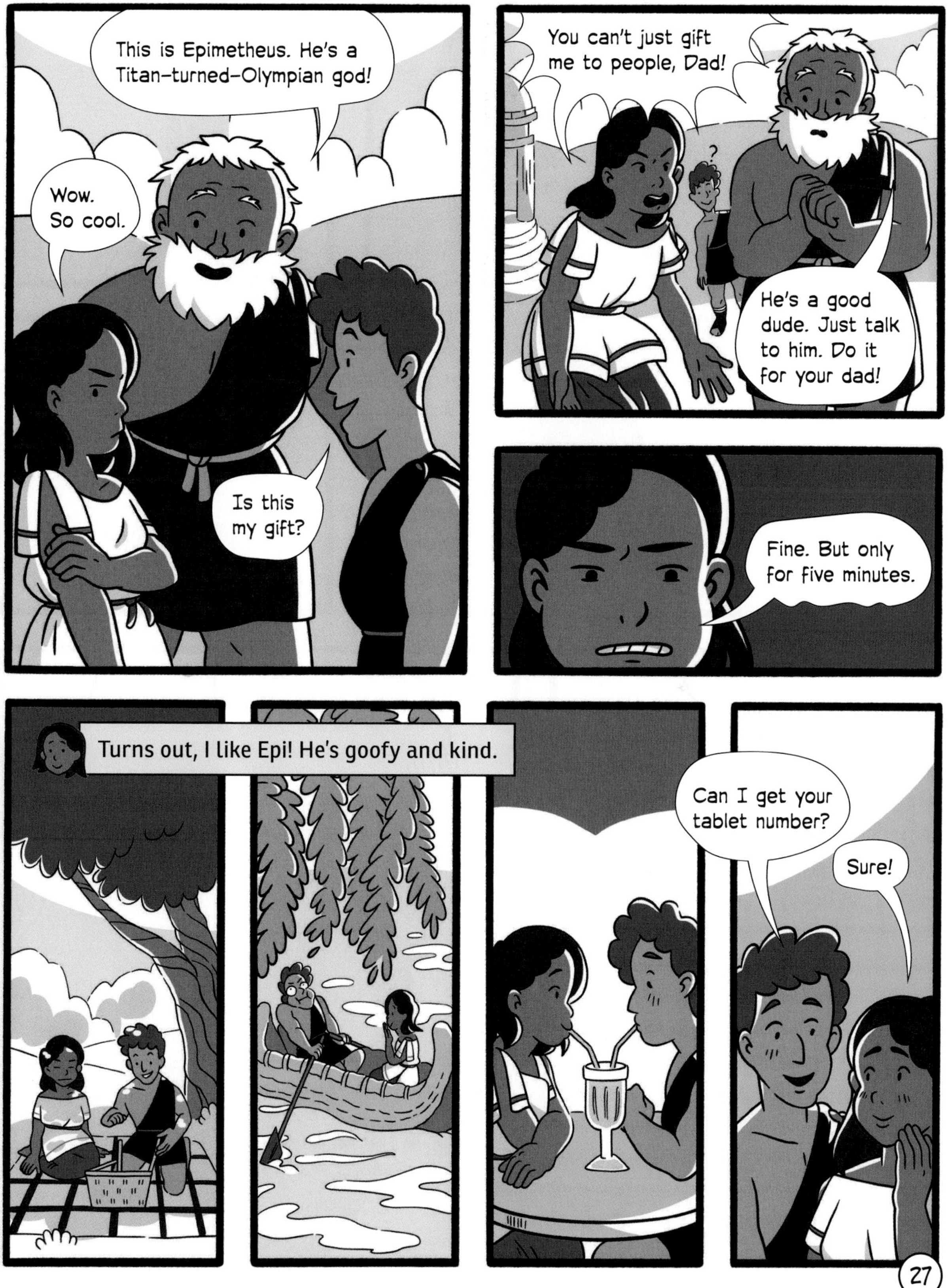
This is Epimetheus. He's a Titan-turned-Olympian god!
Wow. So cool.
Is this my gift?
You can't just gift me to people, Dad!
He's a good dude. Just talk to him. Do it for your dad!
Fine. But only for five minutes.
Turns out, I like Epi! He's goofy and kind.
Can I get your tablet number?
Sure!

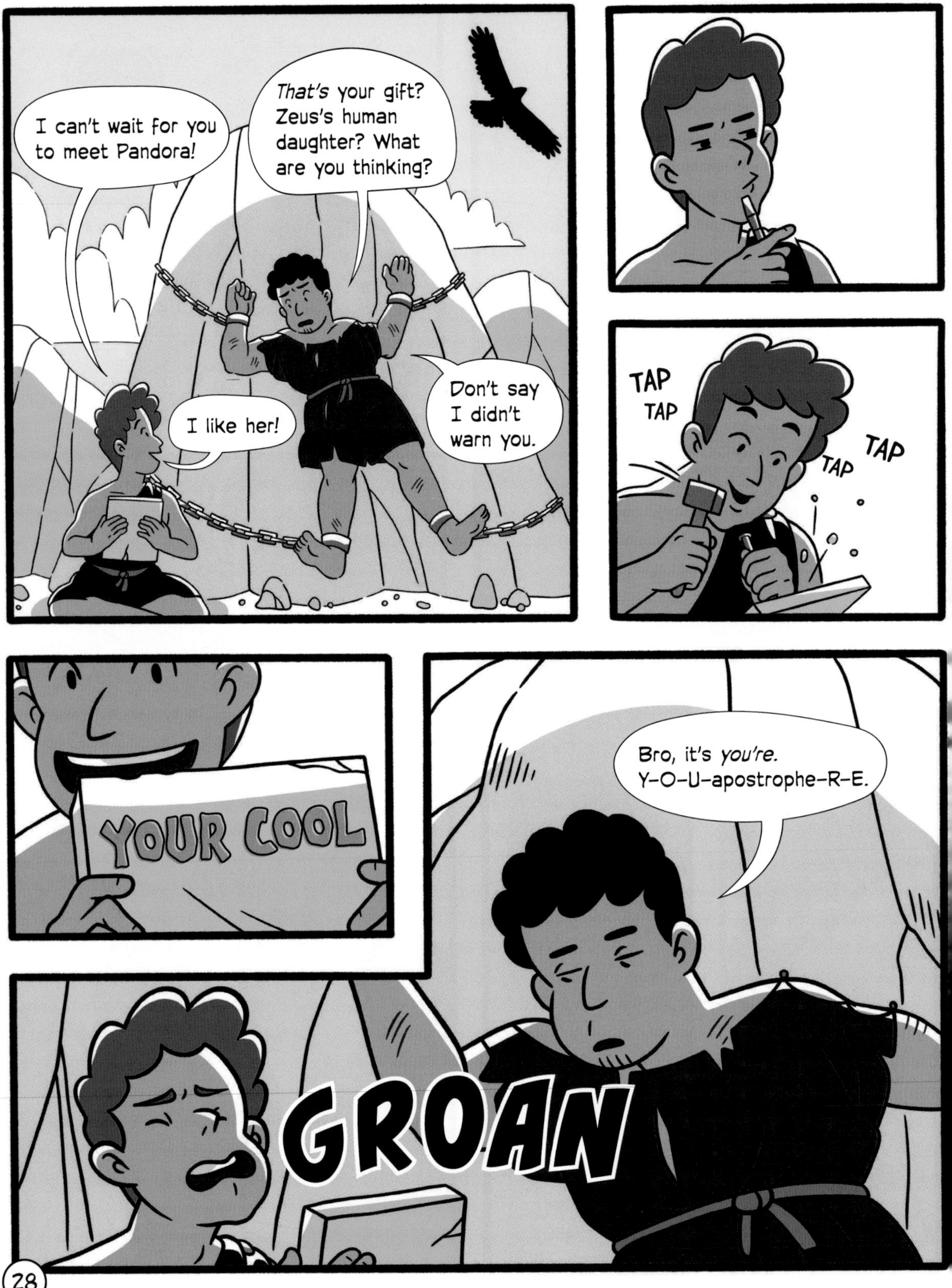
I can't wait for you to meet Pandora!
That's your gift? Zeus's human daughter? What are you thinking?
I like her!
Don't say I didn't warn you.
TAP TAP TAP TAP
YOUR COOL
Bro, it's *you're.* Y-O-U-apostrophe-R-E.
GROAN

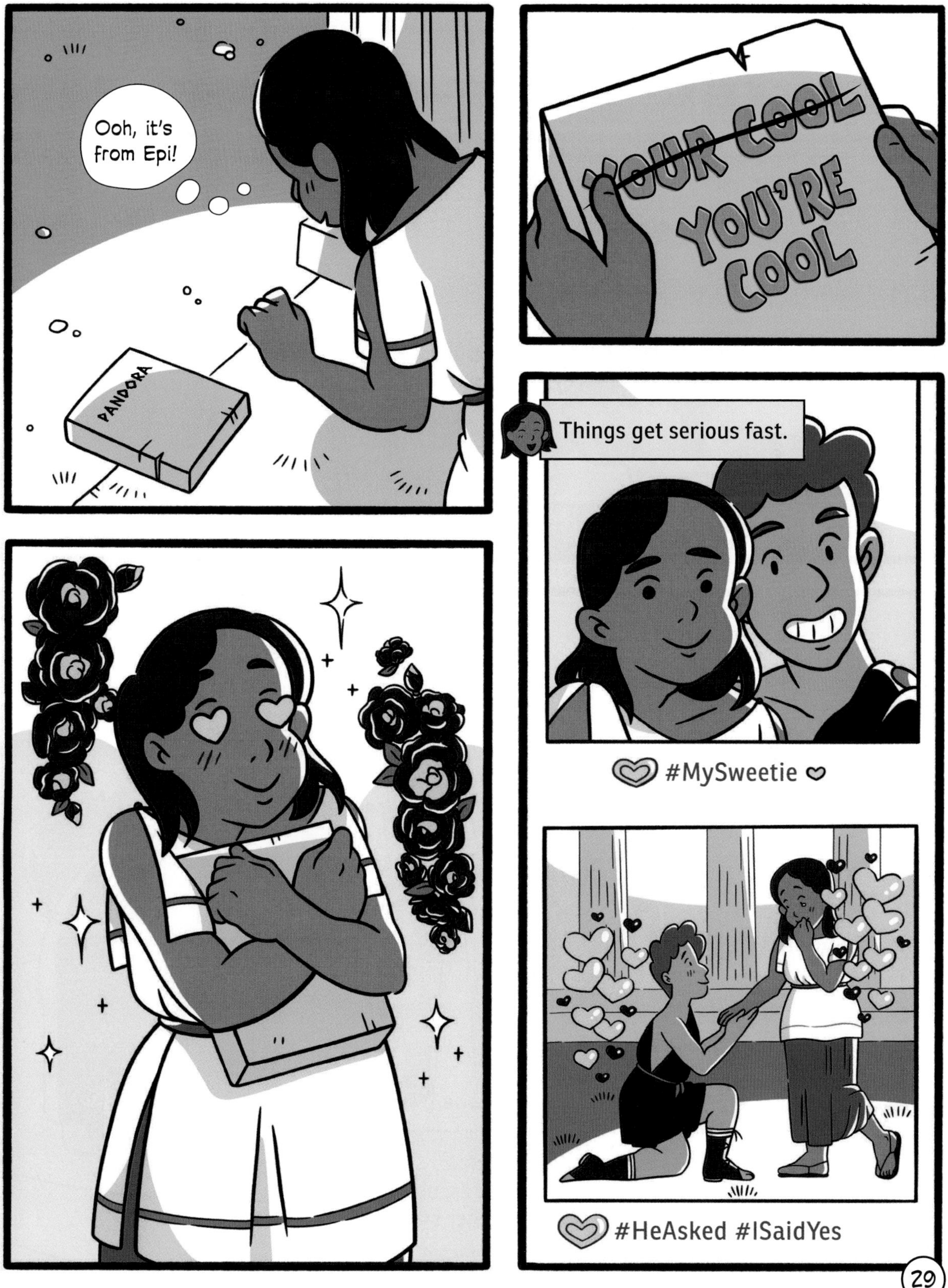
Ooh, it's from Epi!
PANDORA
YOUR COOL
YOU'RE COOL
Things get serious fast.
#MySweetie
#HeAsked #ISaidYes

CHAPTER 5

THE UNOPENED GIFT

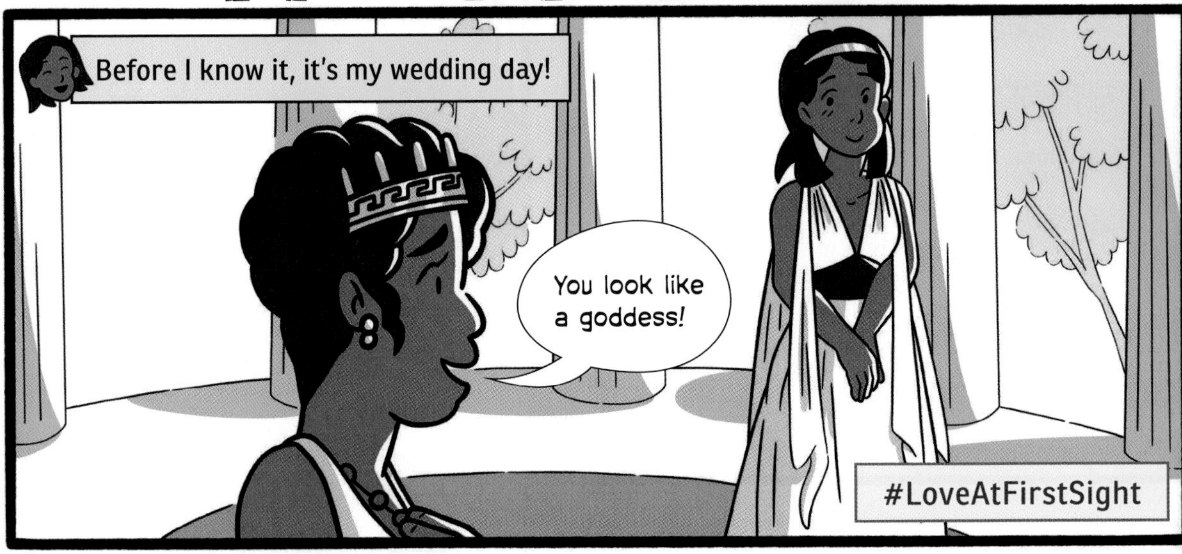

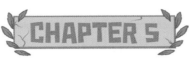

Before I know it, it's my wedding day!
You look like a goddess!
#LoveAtFirstSight

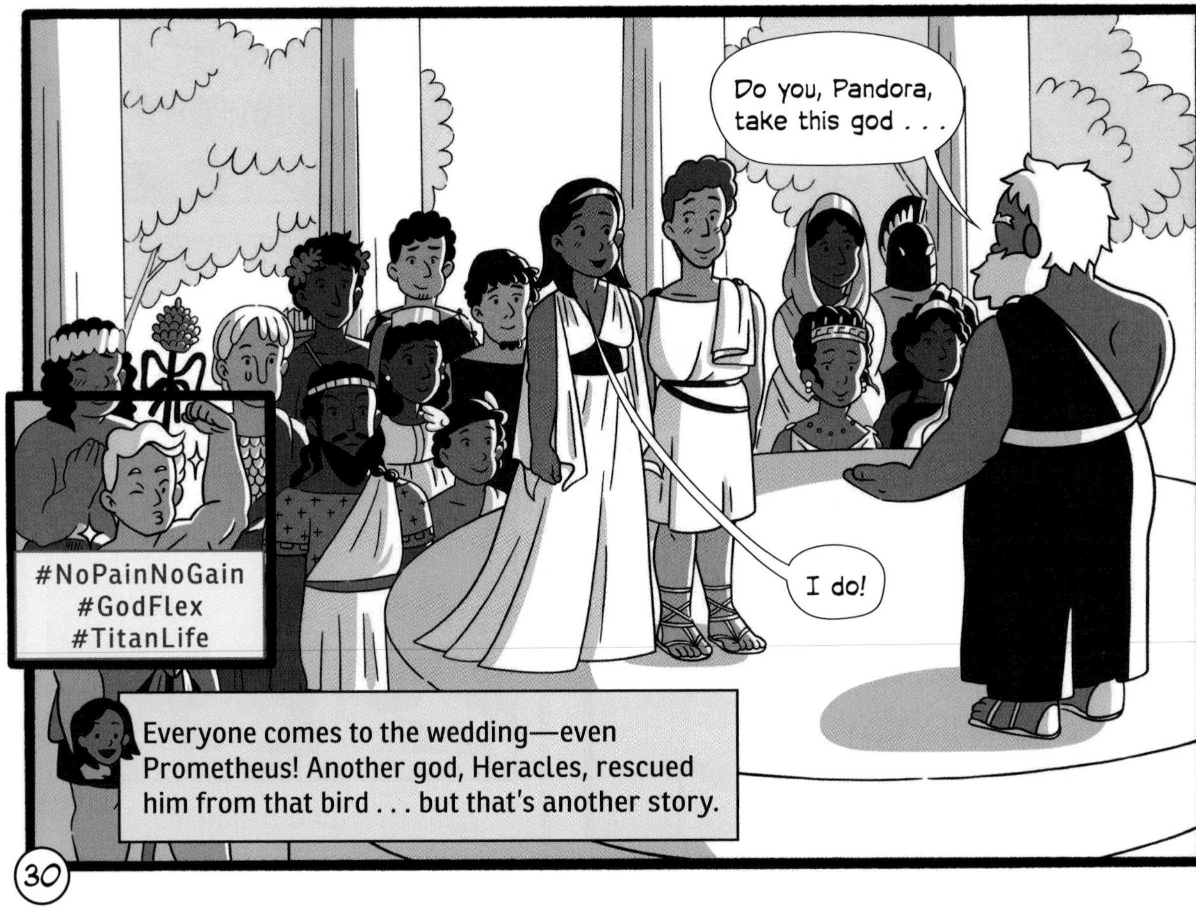

Do you, Pandora, take this god . . .
#NoPainNoGain
#GodFlex
#TitanLife
I do!
Everyone comes to the wedding—even Prometheus! Another god, Heracles, rescued him from that bird . . . but that's another story.

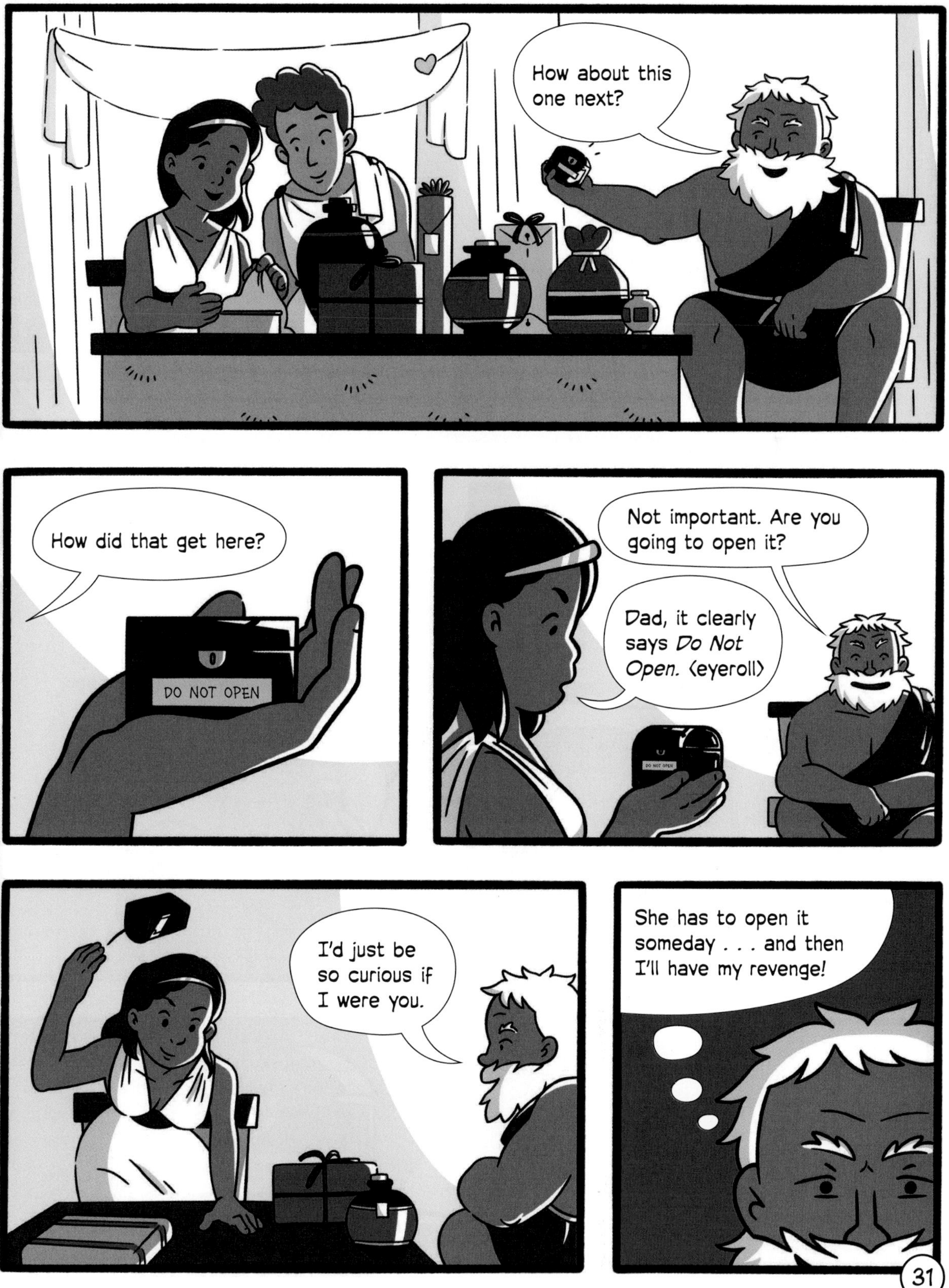
How about this one next?
How did that get here?
DO NOT OPEN
Not important. Are you going to open it?
Dad, it clearly says *Do Not Open.* ⟨eyeroll⟩
DO NOT OPEN
I'd just be so curious if I were you.
She has to open it someday . . . and then I'll have my revenge!

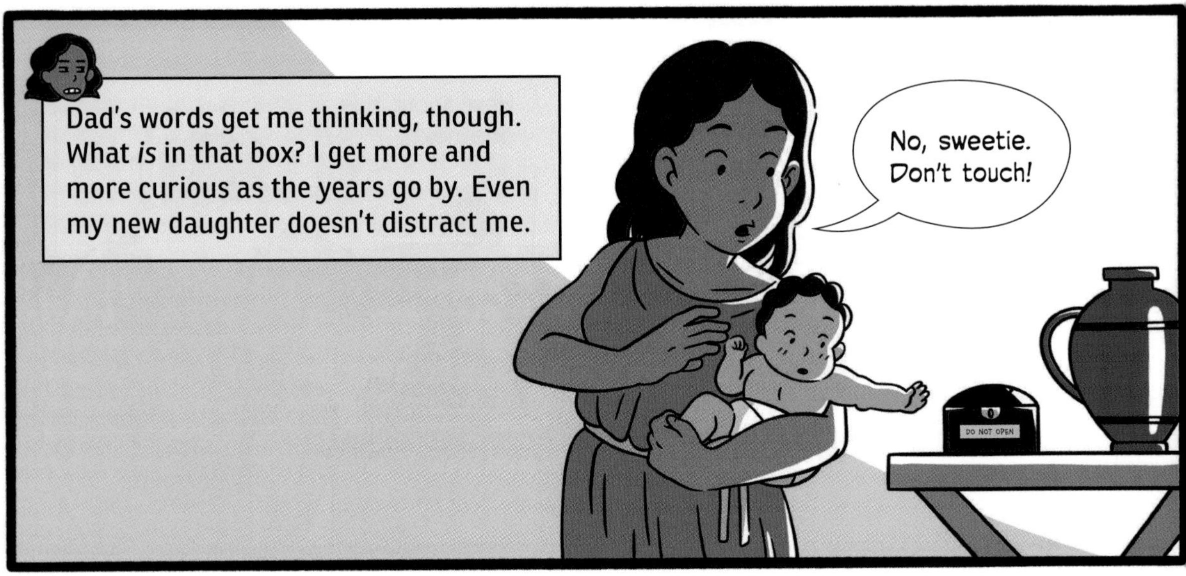
Dad's words get me thinking, though. What *is* in that box? I get more and more curious as the years go by. Even my new daughter doesn't distract me.
No, sweetie. Don't touch!
DO NOT OPEN

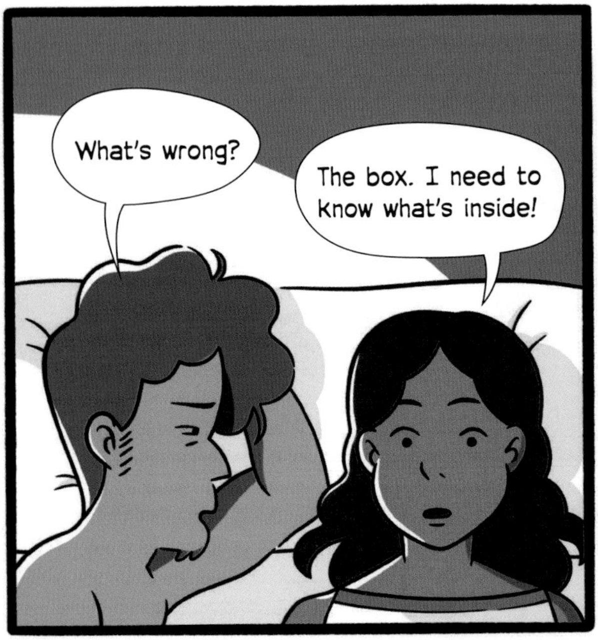
What's wrong?
The box. I need to know what's inside!

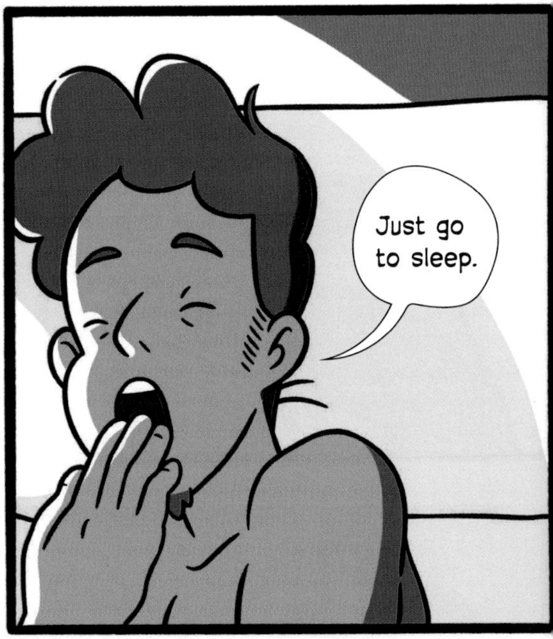
Just go to sleep.

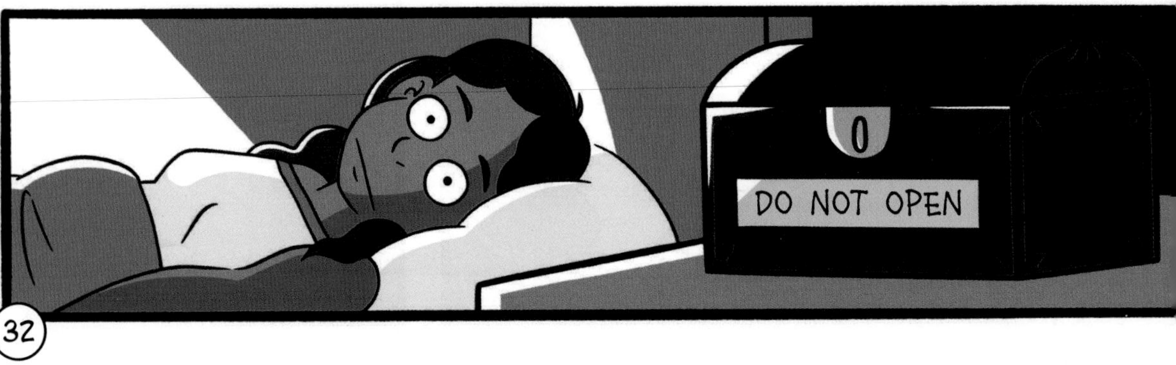
DO NOT OPEN

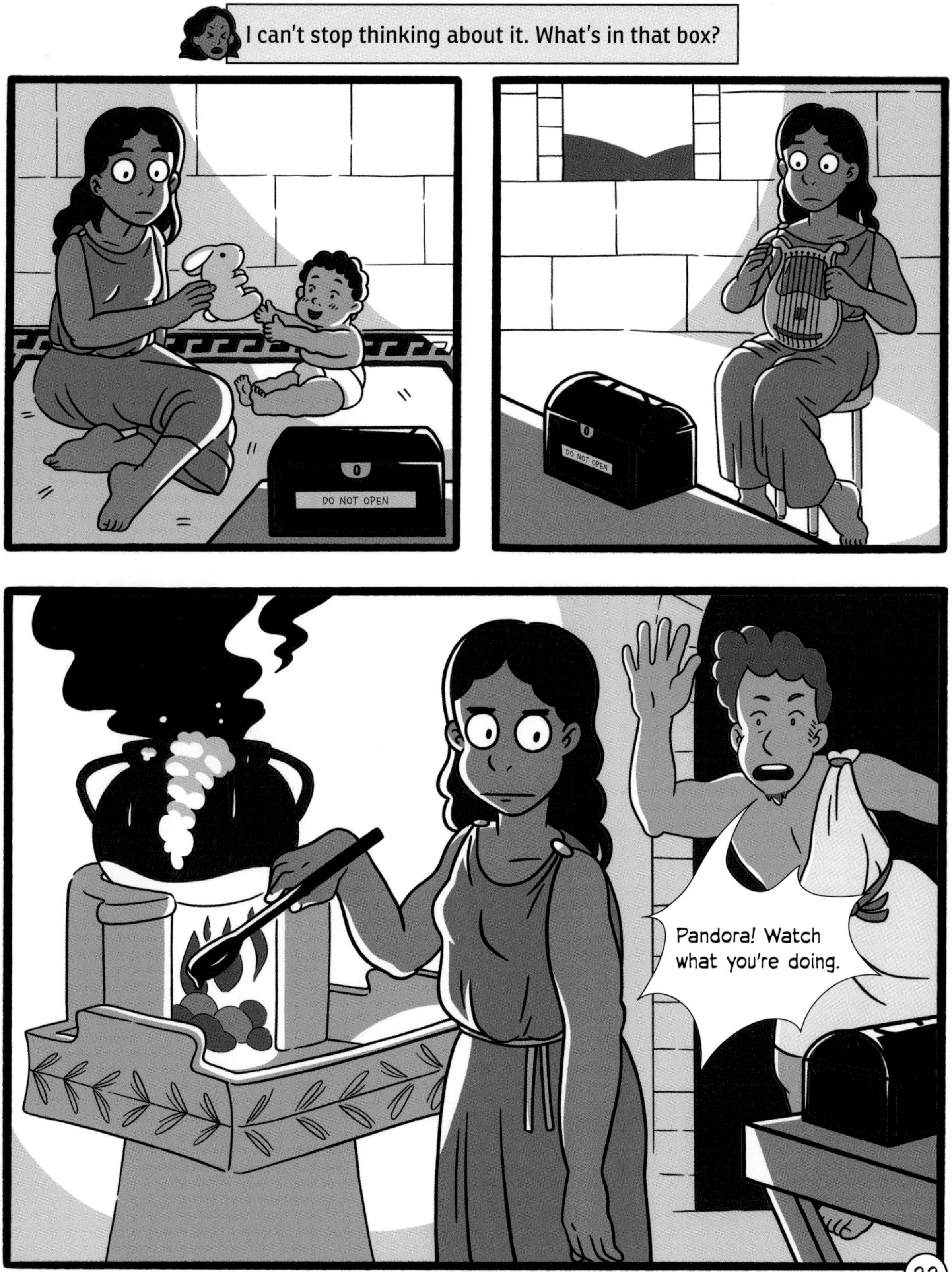
I can't stop thinking about it. What's in that box?
DO NOT OPEN
DO NOT OPEN
Pandora! Watch what you're doing.

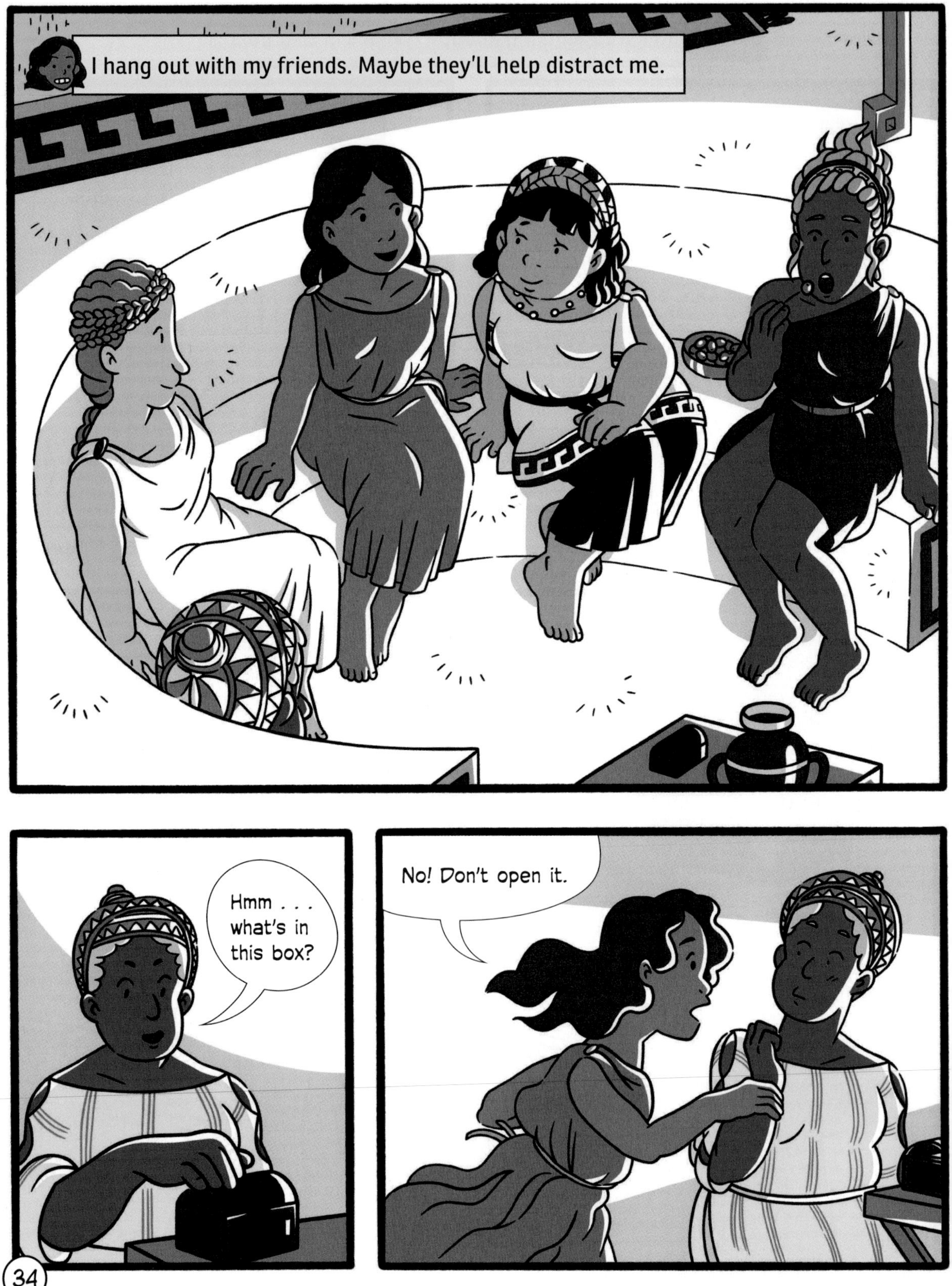
I hang out with my friends. Maybe they'll help distract me.
Hmm . . . what's in this box?
No! Don't open it.

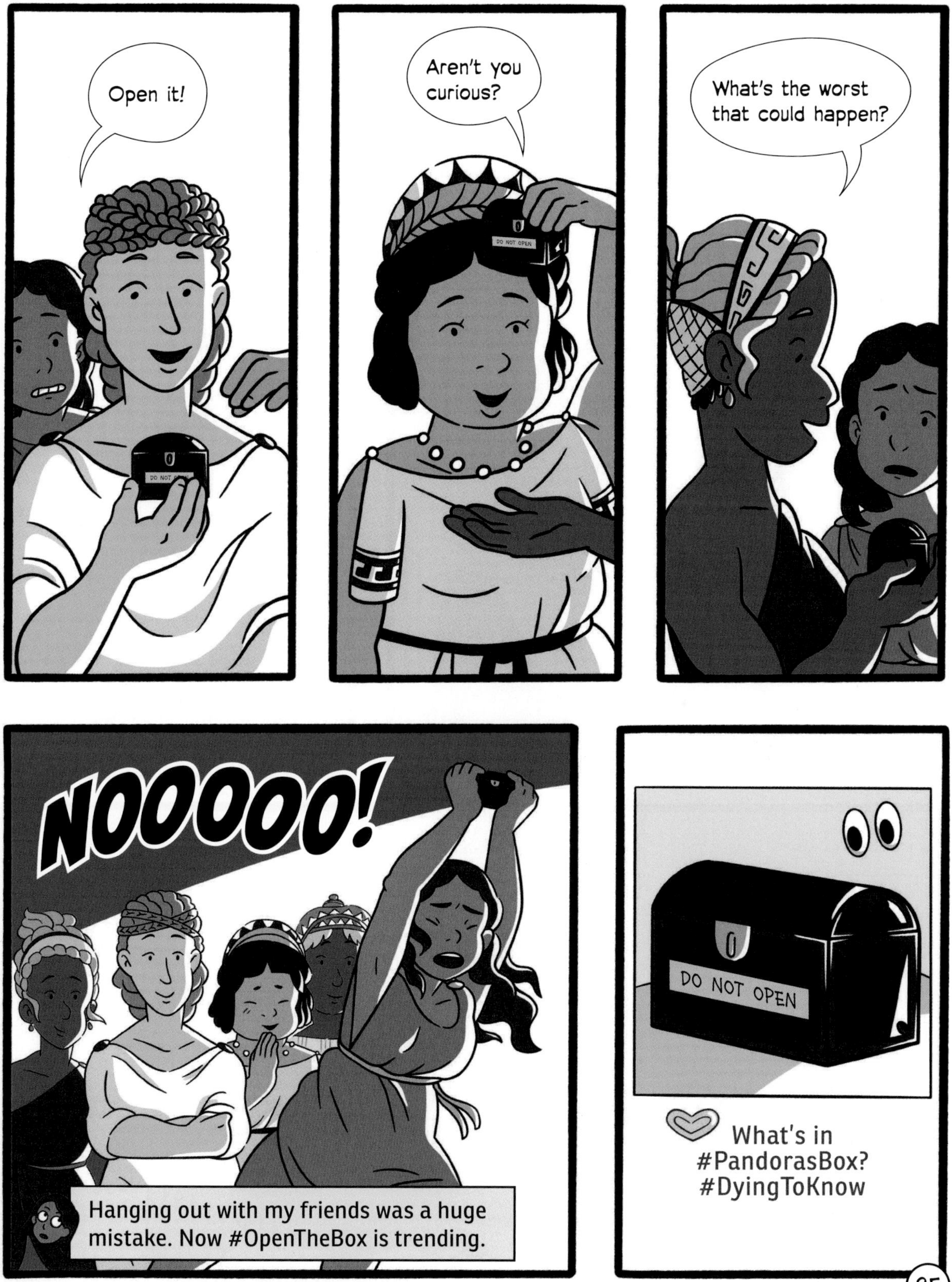
Open it!
Aren't you curious?
DO NOT OPEN
What's the worst that could happen?
NOOOOO!
Hanging out with my friends was a huge mistake. Now #OpenTheBox is trending.
DO NOT OPEN
What's in #PandorasBox? #DyingToKnow

CHAPTER 6

WHAT'S IN THE BOX?

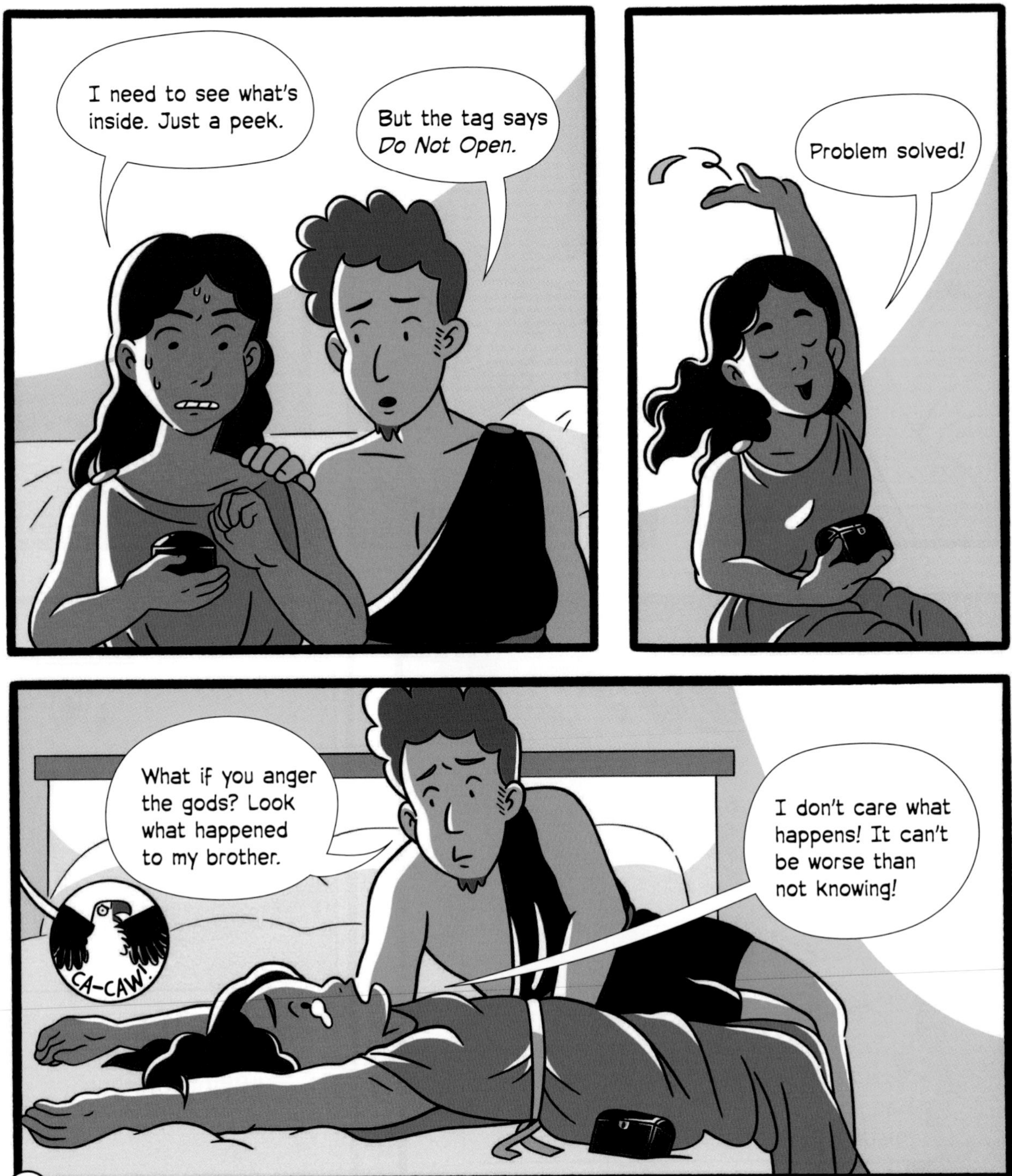

I need to see what's inside. Just a peek.
But the tag says *Do Not Open.*
Problem solved!
What if you anger the gods? Look what happened to my brother.
CA-CAW!
I don't care what happens! It can't be worse than not knowing!

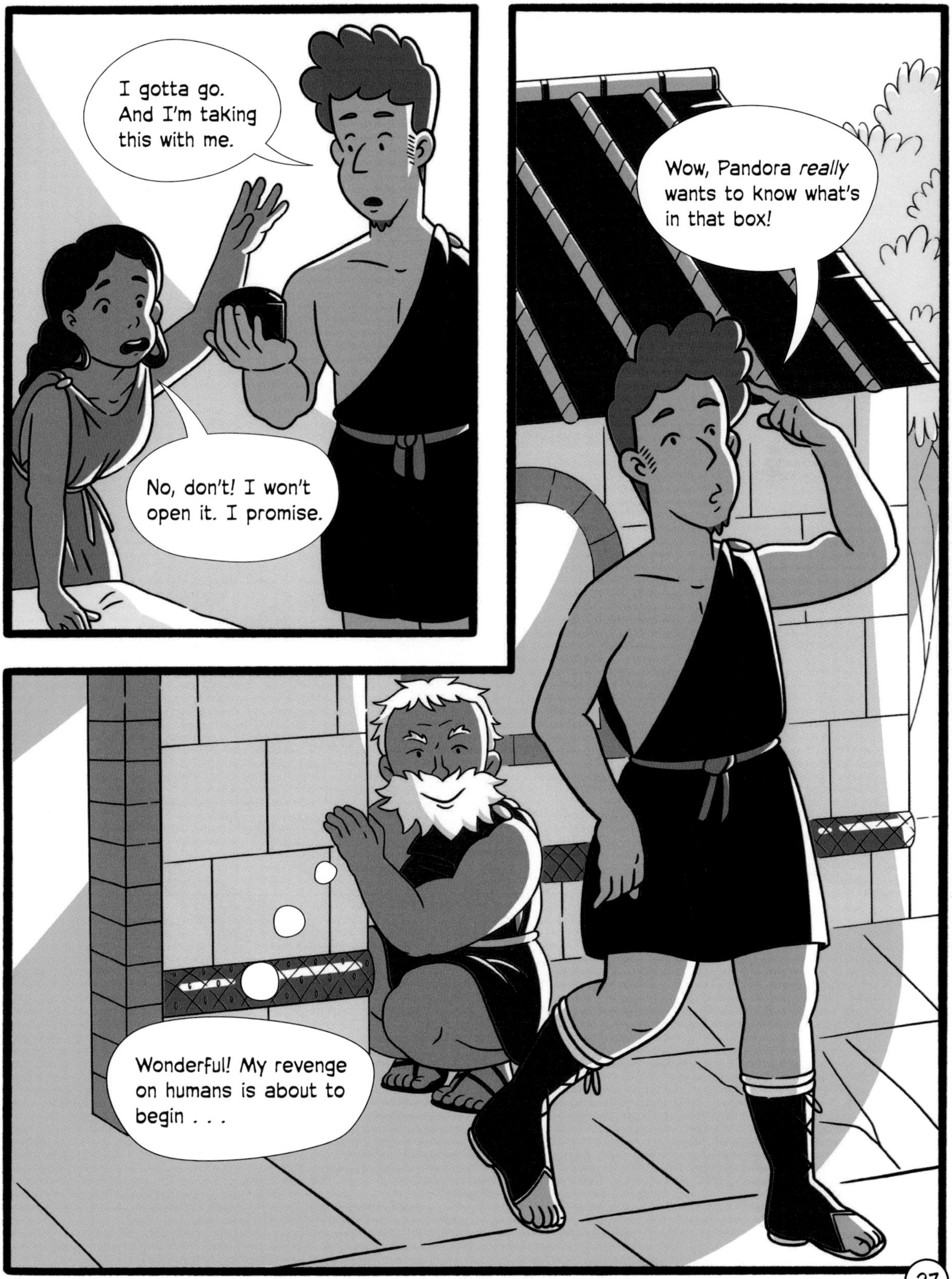

I gotta go. And I'm taking this with me.
No, don't! I won't open it. I promise.
Wow, Pandora *really* wants to know what's in that box!
Wonderful! My revenge on humans is about to begin . . .

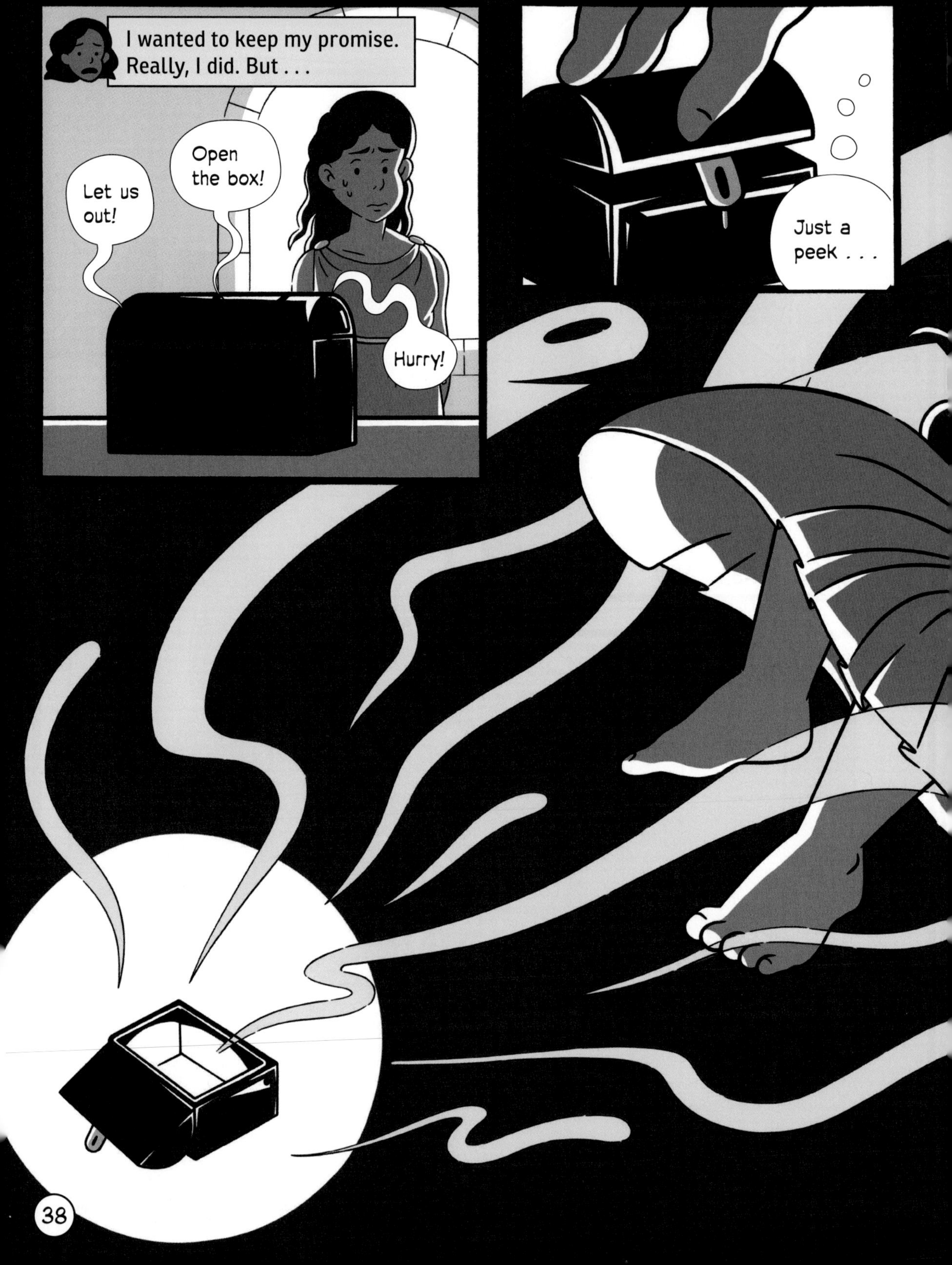
I wanted to keep my promise. Really, I did. But . . .
Let us out!
Open the box!
Hurry!
Just a peek . . .

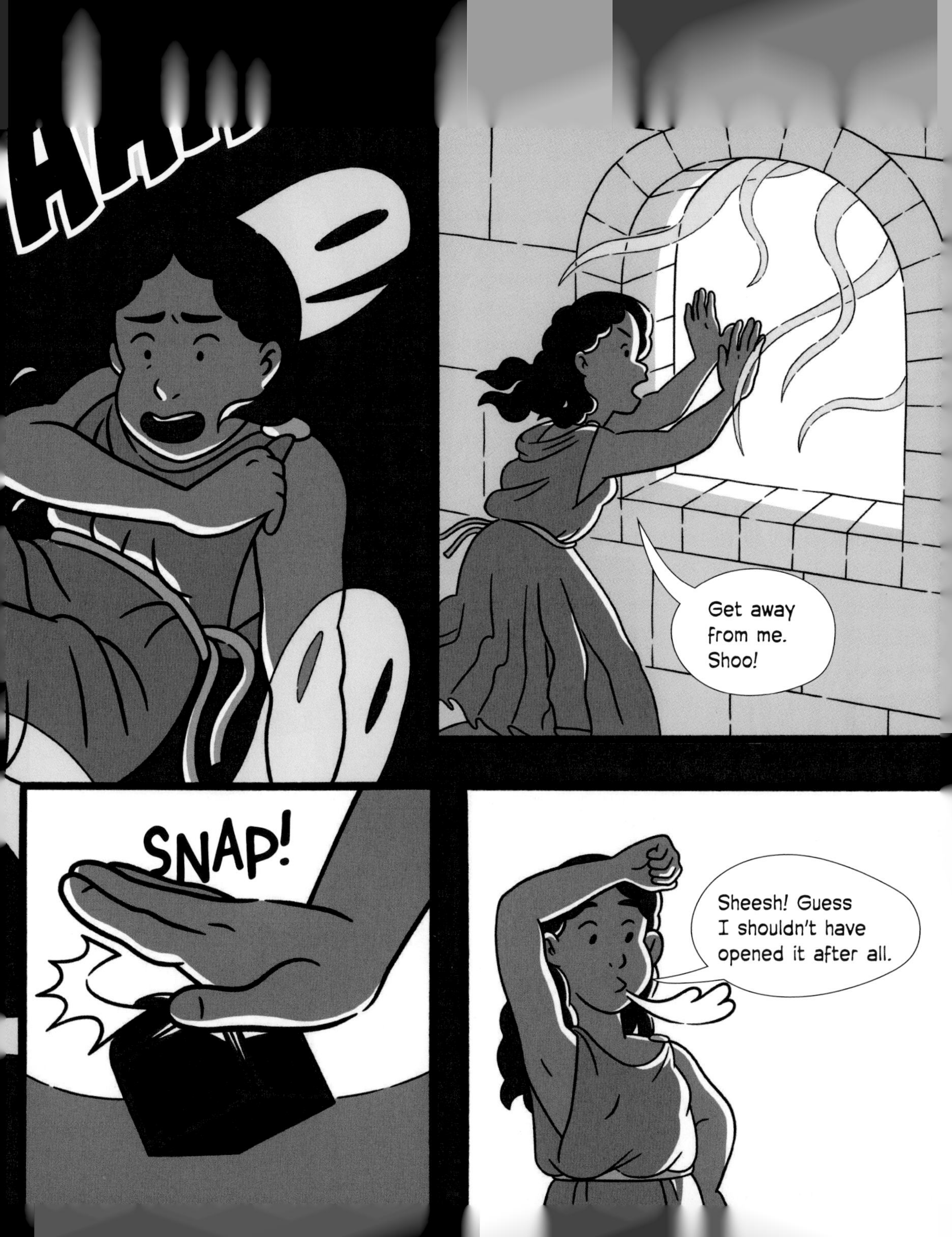
Get away from me. Shoo!
SNAP!
Sheesh! Guess I shouldn't have opened it after all.

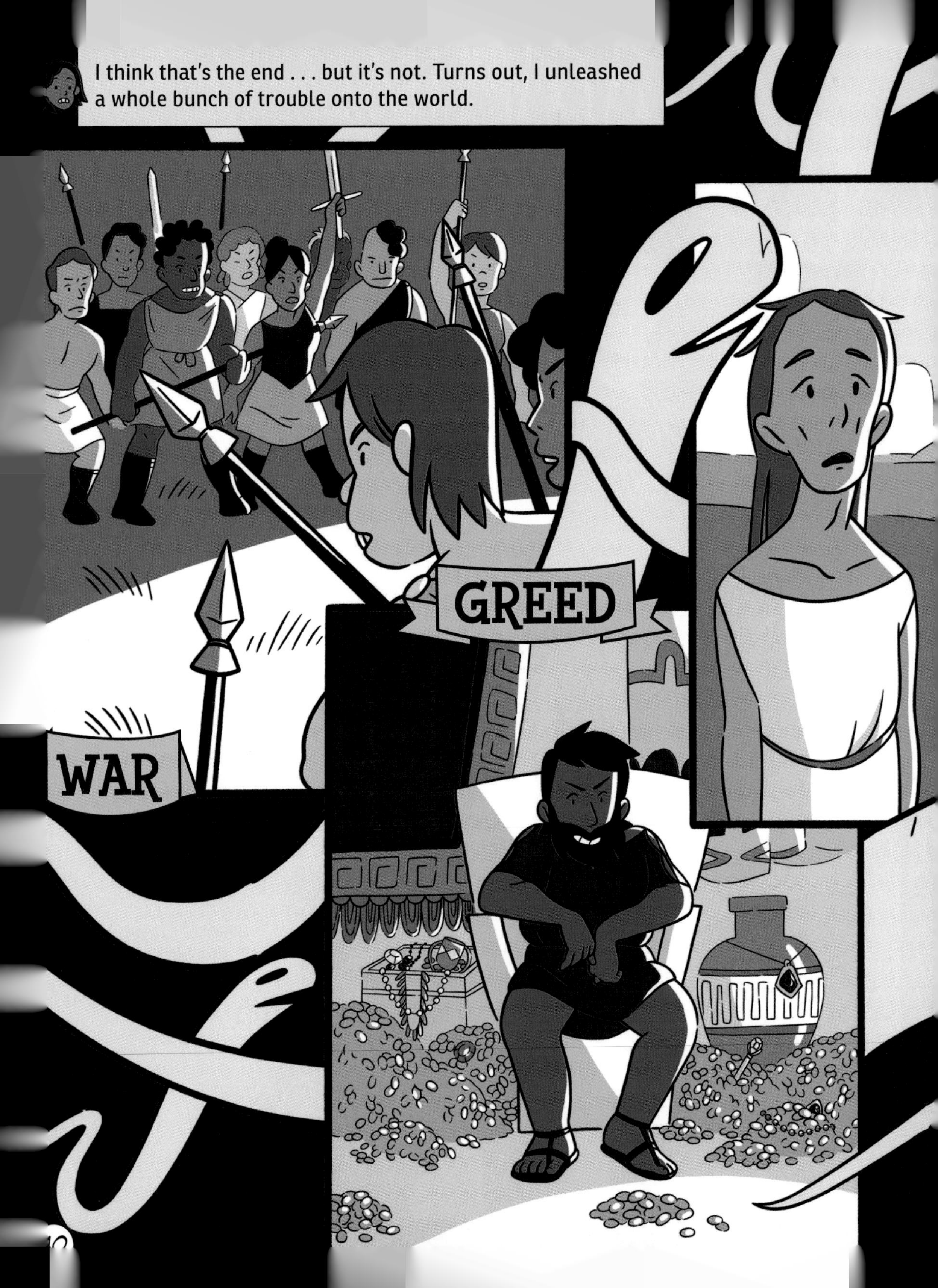
I think that's the end . . . but it's not. Turns out, I unleashed a whole bunch of trouble onto the world.
WAR
GREED

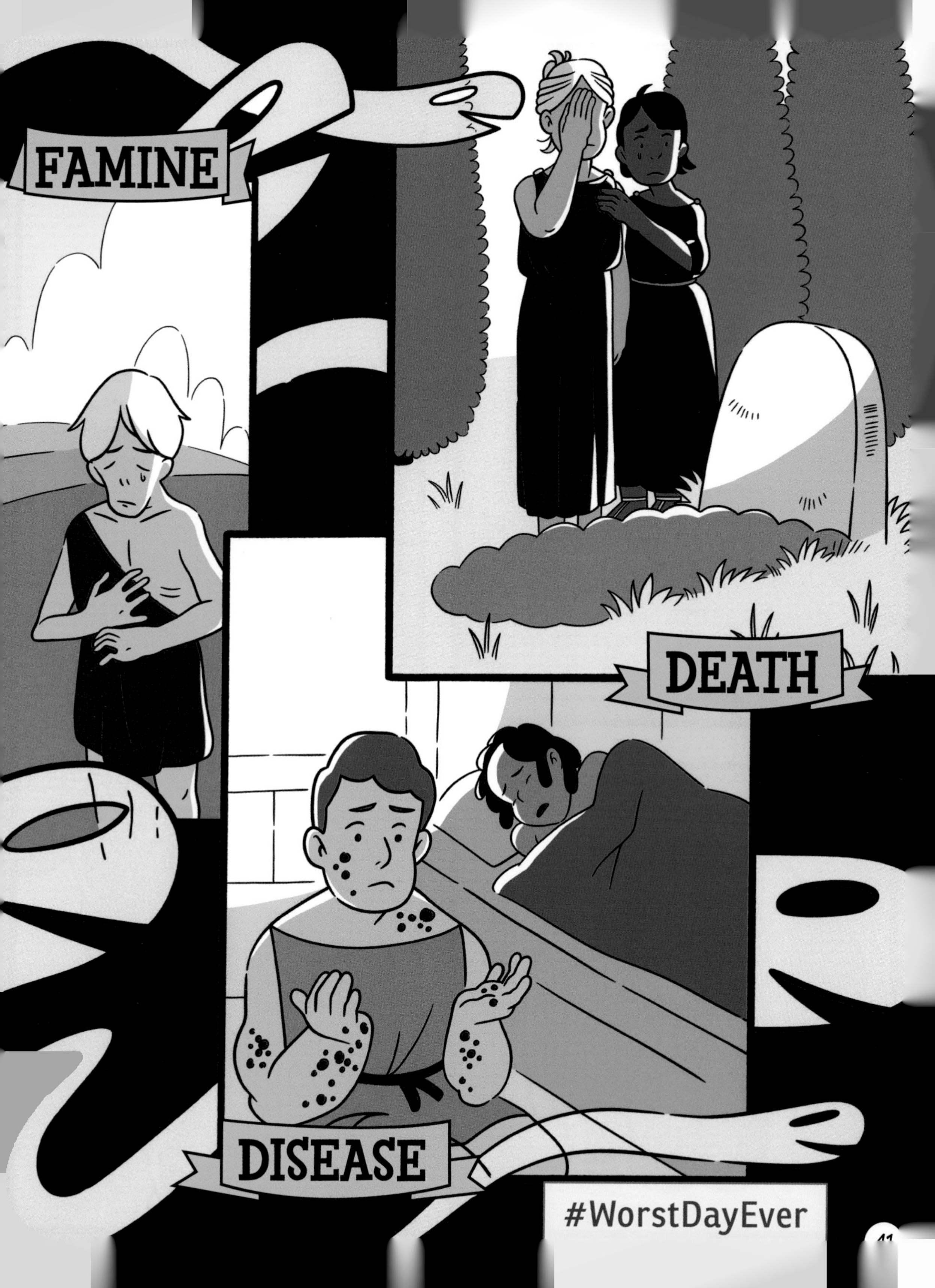
FAMINE
DEATH
DISEASE
#WorstDayEver

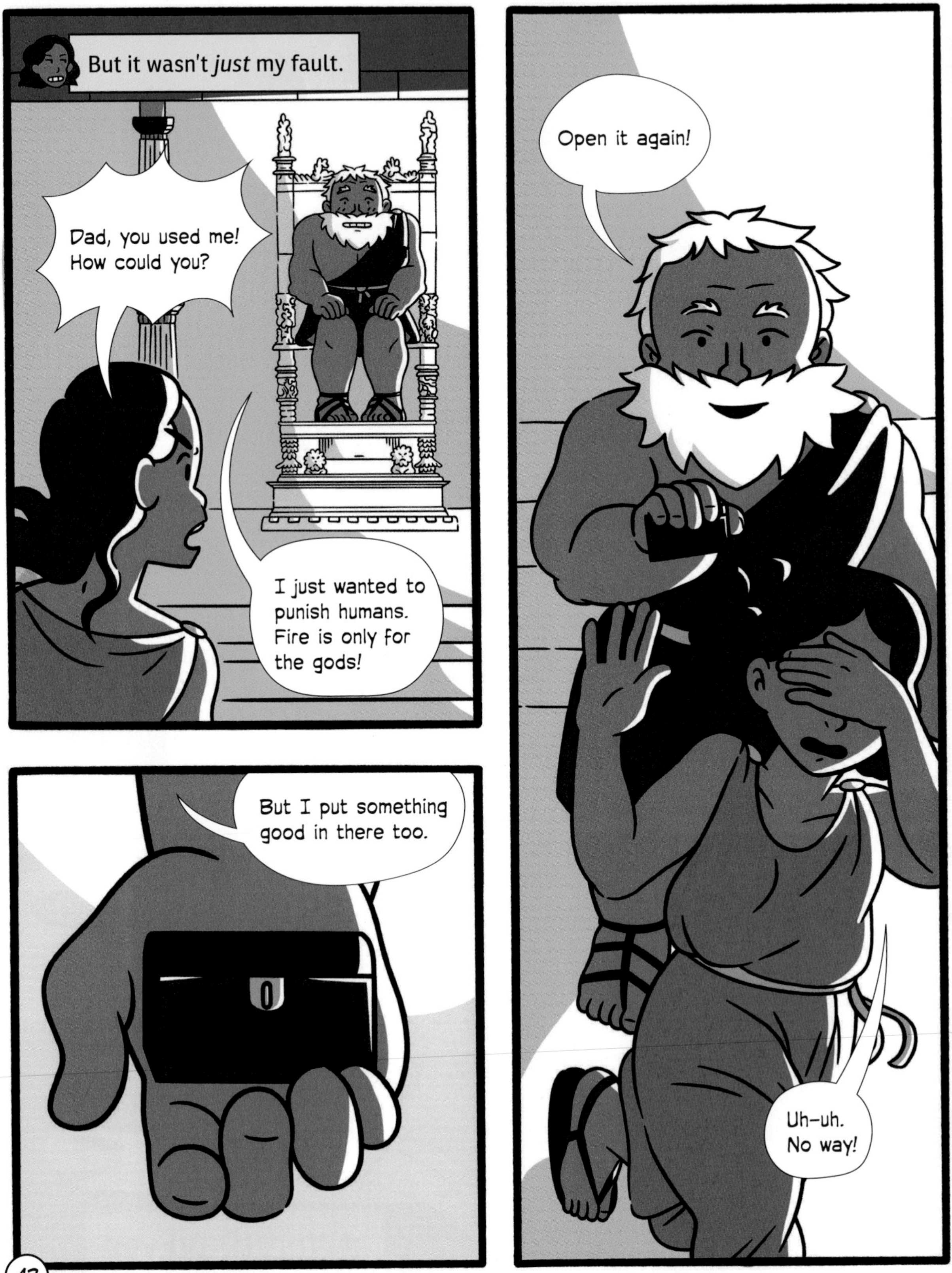
But it wasn't *just* my fault.
Dad, you used me! How could you?
I just wanted to punish humans. Fire is only for the gods!
But I put something good in there too.
Open it again!
Uh-uh. No way!

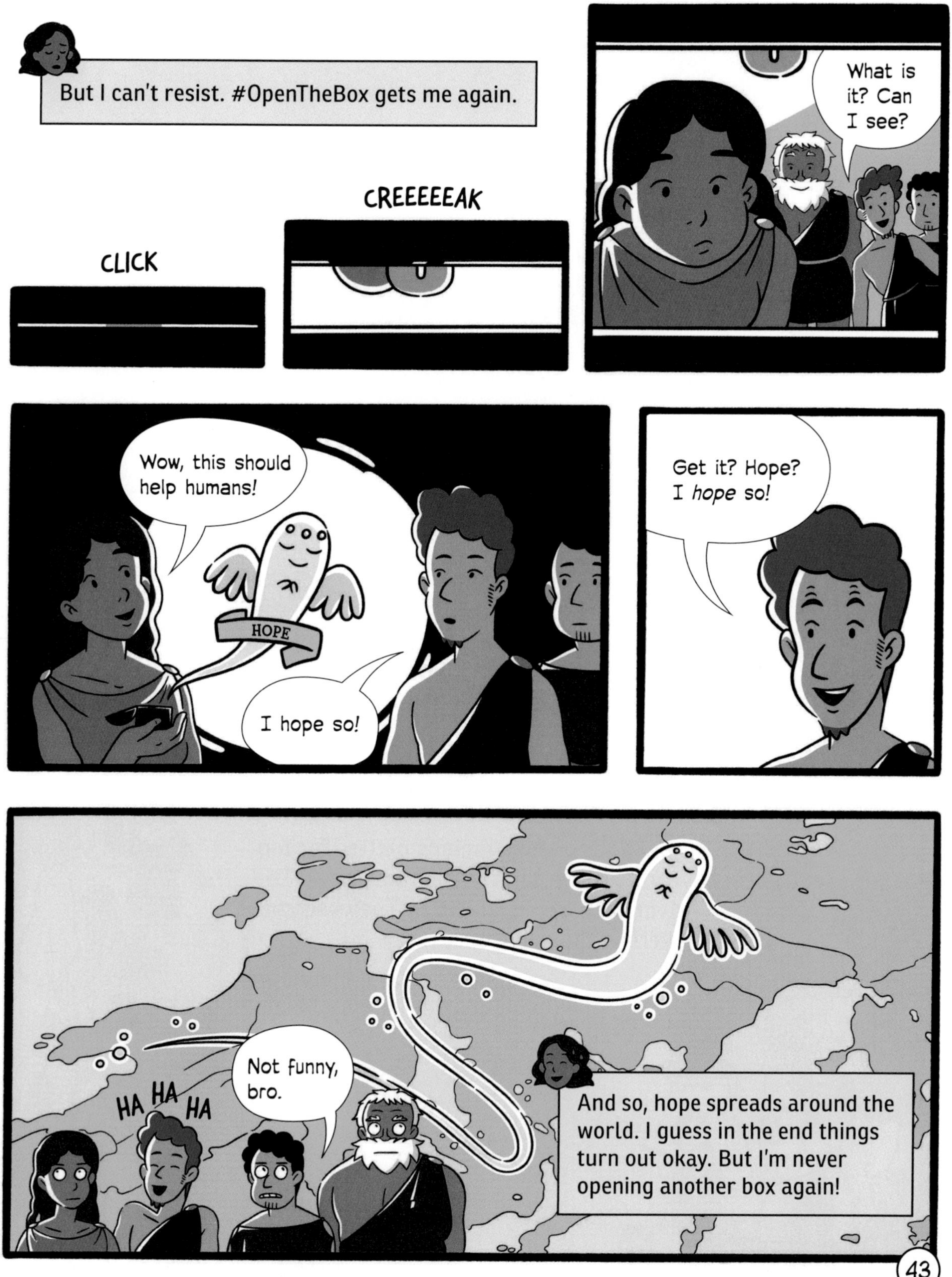
But I can't resist. #OpenTheBox gets me again.
CLICK
CREEEEEAK
What is it? Can I see?
Wow, this should help humans!
HOPE
I hope so!
Get it? Hope? I *hope* so!
HA HA HA
Not funny, bro.
And so, hope spreads around the world. I guess in the end things turn out okay. But I'm never opening another box again!

More About Pandora

In ancient myths, Pandora's box wasn't a box at all—it was a jar. In the sixteenth century, the word was incorrectly translated to "box."

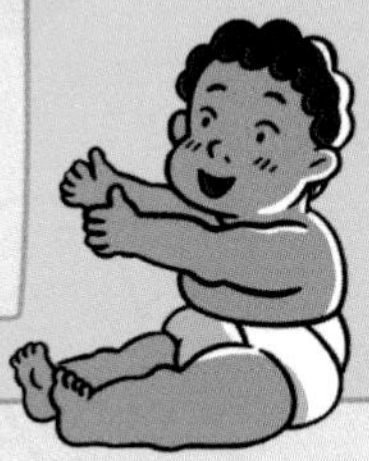

Pandora and Epi had a daughter. She married a son of Zeus. When Zeus flooded Earth in anger, they built a large ship called an ark and survived.

The Titans and Olympians battled for ten years. Prometheus's vision was right. The Olympians were victorious. They became rulers of the universe.

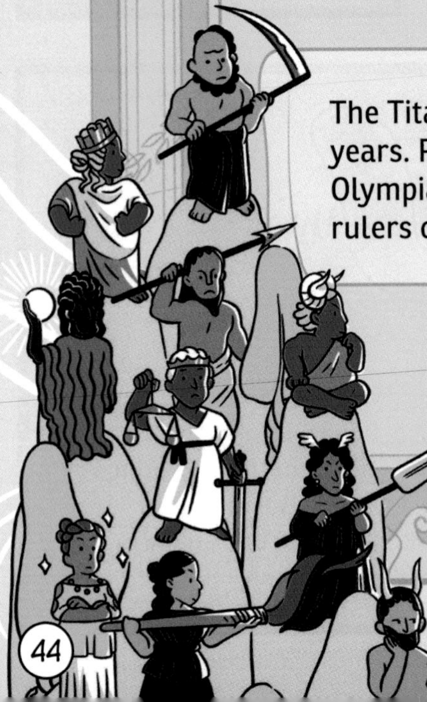

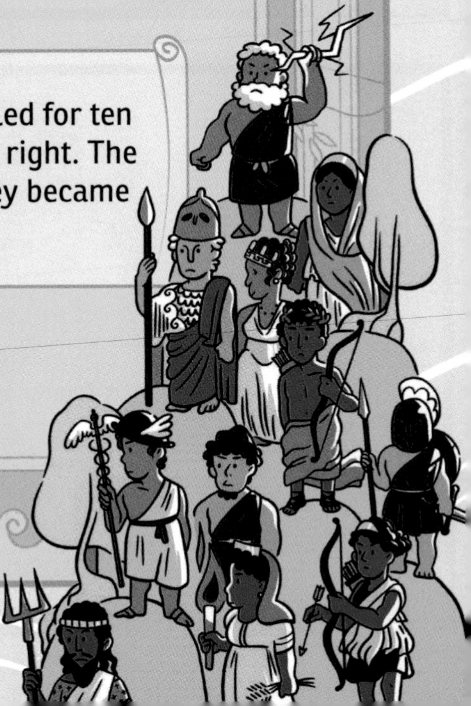

Pandora's image was found on pottery dating back to 5 BCE.

Some versions of Pandora's story say that the box actually contained blessings. When she opened the box, the blessings escaped and were never seen again.

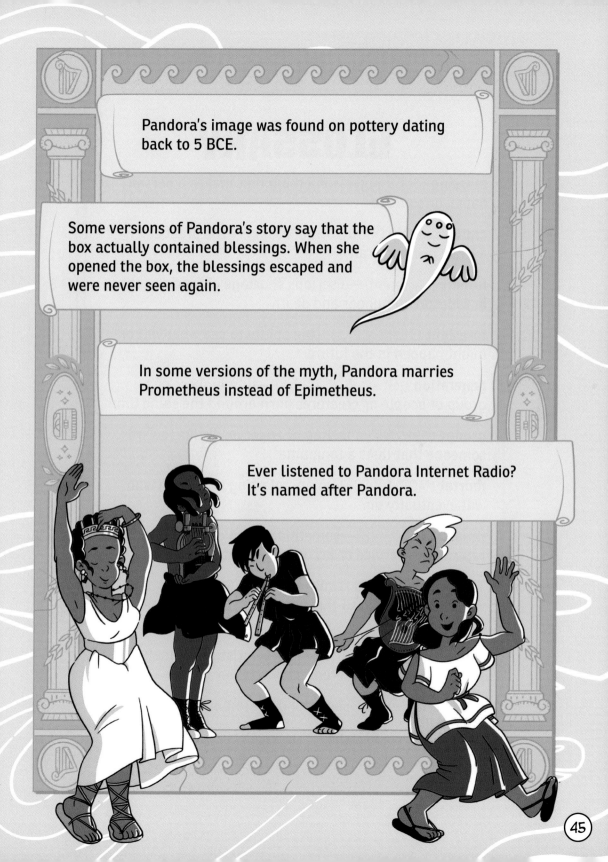

In some versions of the myth, Pandora marries Prometheus instead of Epimetheus.

Ever listened to Pandora Internet Radio? It's named after Pandora.

Glossary

blessing (BLES-ing)—something that makes a person happy or content

craftsmanship (KRAFTS-muhn-ship)—the practice of a trade or handicraft

famine (FA-muhn)—a serious shortage of food resulting in widespread hunger and death

foresight (FAWR-sahyt)—the ability to see what will or might happen in the future

generation (jen-uh-RAY-shuhn)—all members of a group of people or creatures born around the same time

grudge (GRUHJ)—a feeling of anger or dislike toward someone that lasts a long time

mortal (MOR-tuhl)—human, referring to a being who will eventually die

reward (ri-WAWRD)—something given or offered in return for a service or accomplishment

Titan (TAHYT-n)—a family of gods in Greek mythology who ruled Earth until they were overthrown by the Olympians

trait (TRATE)—a quality or characteristic that makes one person or animal different from another

vision (VIZH-uhn)—something dreamt or imagined in the mind

Internet Sites

Britannica: Pandora
britannica.com/topic/Pandora-Greek-mythology

Greek Legends and Myths: Pandora in Greek Mythology
greeklegendsandmyths.com/pandora.html

World History Encyclopedia: Pandora
worldhistory.org/Pandora

Other Books in This Series

MYTHOLOGY GRAPHICS
PERSEPHONE AND THE UNDERWORLD

MYTHOLOGY GRAPHICS
THE TROJAN HORSE

MYTHOLOGY GRAPHICS
THE TWELVE LABORS OF HERCULES

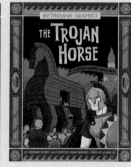

ABOUT THE CREATORS

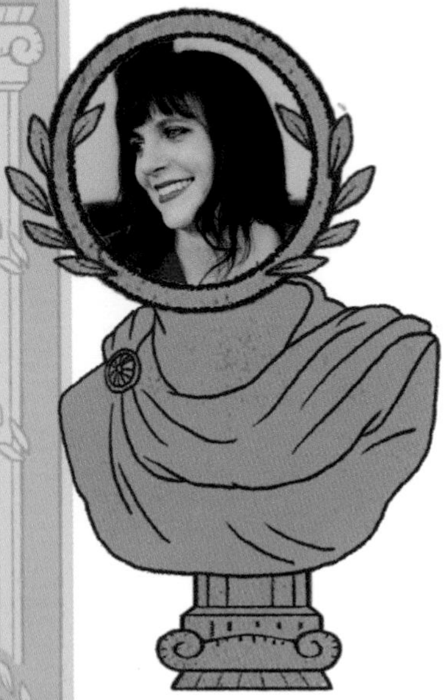

Jessica Gunderson grew up in the small town of Washburn, North Dakota. She has a bachelor's degree from the University of North Dakota and an MFA in Creative Writing from Minnesota State University, Mankato. She has written more than 75 books for young readers. Her book *President Lincoln's Killer and the America He Left Behind* won a 2018 Eureka! Nonfiction Children's Book Silver Award. She currently lives in Madison, Wisconsin.

Photo Credit: Anda Marie Photography

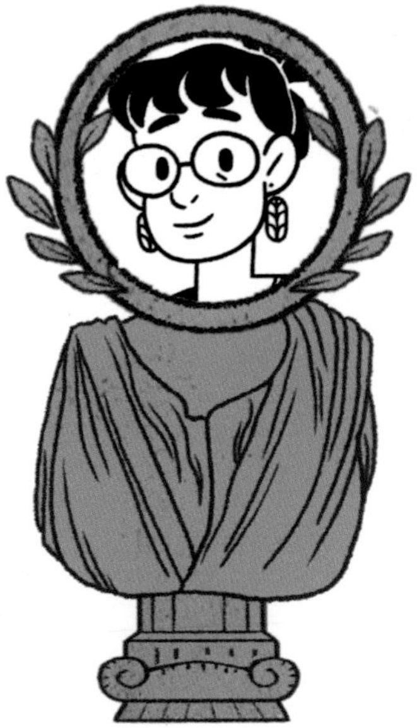

Jessi Zabarsky is a cartoonist and illustrator living in Chicago, Illinois. She makes comics about girls, magic, big feelings, and fantastic worlds. Her first two graphic novels, *Witchlight* and *Coming Back*, are available from Random House Graphic. She has stopped counting her houseplants, as there are now far too many.

Image Credit: Jessi Zabarsky

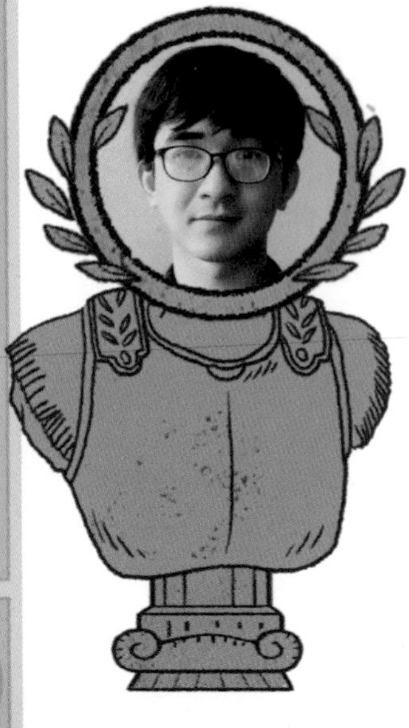

Le Nhat Vu was born in Nha Trang, a seaside city in Vietnam. He now works as a book illustrator in Ho Chi Minh City. He draws inspiration from fantasy, adventure, and poetic stories. During his free time, he enjoys reading Japanese comics (manga) and novels as well as watching football and movies—maybe with a cup of milk coffee.

Photo Credit: Le Nhat Vu